The Government Debt Iceberg

The Government Debt Iceberg

JAGADEESH GOKHALE

iea

The Institute of Economic Affairs

First published in Great Britain in 2014 by
The Institute of Economic Affairs
2 Lord North Street
Westminster
London SW1P 3LB
in association with London Publishing Partnership Ltd
www.londonpublishingpartnership.co.uk

The mission of the Institute of Economic Affairs is to improve public understanding of the fundamental institutions of a free society, with particular reference to the role of markets in solving economic and social problems.

A CIP catalogue record for this book is available from the British Library.

ISBN 978-0-255-36666-3

Many IEA publications are translated into languages other
than English or are reprinted. Permission to translate or to reprint
should be sought from the Director General at the address above.

Typeset in Kepler by T&T Productions Ltd
www.tandtproductions.com

Printed and bound in Great Britain by Page Bros

CONTENTS

THE AUTHOR

Jagadeesh Gokhale is Senior Fellow at the Cato Institute, Washington, DC, and a Member of the United States' Social Security Advisory Board. The author's past positions include senior economic advisor to the Federal Reserve Bank of Cleveland, consultant at the US Department of the Treasury, and visiting scholar at the American Enterprise Institute. He holds a doctorate in economics from Boston University.

FOREWORD

Not long before writing this, the euro zone was still in crisis. Across the Atlantic, all the focus of attention is on whether there can be a short-term fix to allow the US government to continue with its current policies. In the EU, there are widespread concerns – perhaps unmerited – about whether reductions in government borrowing will plunge the euro zone into further recession. The one constant, however, is that, in good times and in bad, governments throughout the West have adopted policies that impose huge fiscal burdens on future generations.

Even when countries appear to have prudent fiscal policies according to short-term government borrowing and debt metrics, they are normally building up future commitments that do not appear on the government's balance sheet and will not involve actual cash payments for decades. For example, if the government borrows £50,000 to pay the salary of one extra teacher this year, then that additional indebtedness will be clear to taxpayers and securities markets alike. But, if the government makes a commitment to pay future pensions that have a present value of £50,000 and which involve exactly the same future cash flows as servicing the debt issued to finance the additional teacher, there will be no additional borrowing recorded.

However, the commitment to pay the future pension may be just as binding as the commitment to service government debt. Indeed, in some circumstances, such as the case of contractual commitments to pay future pensions to public sector workers, a pension promise may have a higher legal status than government debt.

In this IEA Research Monograph on inter-generational accounting, the author, Jagadeesh Gokhale, points out that existing metrics of government debt are entirely backward looking. If a government has accumulated debt of 85 per cent of national income, that simply tells you something about past cash flows. The figure tells you nothing at all about those commitments the government has made that involve future cash flows. If a private insurance company promised to pay out £3 billion of annuities over the next 30 years and did not include them on its balance sheet, it would be closed down. Yet this is precisely how the government does its accounting.

When they are calculated, it is common for economists to try to express future government commitments as a percentage of national income. Thus, for example, authors have previously written for the IEA suggesting that total public sector pension liabilities are around 100 per cent of UK national income and the Office for National Statistics also publishes similar calculations relating to unfunded government commitments. Gokhale argues that expressing such liabilities as a proportion of current annual national income is not appropriate, though it can provide a useful rough and ready measure. Instead, Gokhale looks at the policy changes that would have to be made in order to ensure that the fiscal position was sustainable. For example, under certain assumptions, there would have to be an immediate doubling of federal income taxes in the US to ensure that, on a long-term basis, US federal government revenues will be sufficient to cover government spending commitments. If doubling taxes reduces incomes and revenues, the required tax increase would have to be even steeper. In the EU, all taxes would have to be raised by 13.5 per cent of GDP – a huge figure given that the base for most taxes is much less than the whole of GDP and taxes are already very high – if all future spending commitments are going to be financed by future taxation. Alternatively, of course, future spending plans could be scaled back, though this may be politically just as difficult as increasing taxes, at least in the short term. If no way is eventually found to make such fiscal adjustments, sovereign defaults on explicit debt and implicit pension liabilities must ensue.

The underlying problem is that successive governments have made promises which can simply not be honoured from the existing tax base. The electorate is grazing a fiscal commons at the expense of future generations. Gokhale argues that one step towards changing policy is proper accounting. Other policy changes will then be needed to ensure that, when commitments are made, they are properly funded – probably through private saving.

This IEA Research Monograph is hugely important for the public debate. In modern democracies people of voting age have voted themselves benefits to be paid for, not by sacrifices that they make through funded provision, but by sacrifices that will be made by the next generation of taxpayers, who may not have even been born when the benefits were promised. Arguably, this is one of the most important issues of our time. It is not clear that those democracies that are already close to their taxable capacity will find a way through these problems without reneging on promises. These problems just serve to illustrate how 'present oriented' the modern social welfare state is: while families leave bequests for their children, the same people vote to leave their children Social Security and health care debts.

Inter-generational modelling is a complex subject and the author is to be commended for producing this IEA publication, which explains how we should understand and begin to address the unsustainable burdens we are leaving to the next generation through unfunded government health and pension commitments. This kind of modelling is a necessary first step towards better understanding available policy alternatives for resolving fiscal burdens – to promote a properly framed public debate on the future course of action to take.

PHILIP BOOTH
Editorial and Programme Director
Institute of Economic Affairs
Professor of Insurance and Risk Management
Cass Business School, City University, London
February 2014

The views expressed in this monograph are, as in all IEA publications, those of the author and not those of the Institute (which has no corporate view), its managing trustees, Academic Advisory Council members or senior staff. Neither do they reflect the views of the United States' Social Security Advisory Board, of which the author is a member. With some exceptions, such as with the publication of lectures, all IEA monographs are blind peer-reviewed by at least two academics or researchers who are experts in the field.

ACKNOWLEDGEMENT AND NOTE ON SOURCES

In preparing this monograph for the Institute of Economic Affairs, the United States' Congressional Budget Office's ten-year budget projections from March 2012 were extended and several micro-data sources were used to construct government spending and receipt projections for the United States. Information from Eurostat and the European Income and Living Conditions survey is used to make projections for 25 European Union countries. Official long-range economic assumptions and historical trends of productivity growth and interest rates are used to construct fiscal and generational imbalance estimates. Provision by the Social Security Administration's Felicitie Bell of US population projections and underlying demographic assumptions used in the Social Security trustees' 2012 annual report, responses by CBO officials to the author's clarifying questions on the CBO's federal budget accounting conventions and data provision and formatting assistance from the UK Data Archive are gratefully acknowledged. The author thanks David Schoenbrod for very useful comments and Erin Partin for excellent research assistance.

SUMMARY

- Europe and the United States will soon begin to encounter fiscal constraints the like of which we have never seen before. Federal debt as a percentage of GDP more than doubled between 2000 and 2012. According to the US Congressional Budget Office, total national debt is expected to remain close to 100 per cent of GDP during the next decade and begin to increase thereafter as the baby-boomers fully enter retirement.
- Debt levels in European Union countries have surged similarly, from 60 per cent of national income during the mid 2000s to 85 per cent of national income today.
- An ageing population alone does not create greater government indebtedness as long as each generation sets aside adequate funds to meet their own future pensions and health-care costs. Instead of adopting such pre-funded retirement support systems, however, Western governments have developed unfunded social insurance programmes where retiree benefits are paid for from the taxes of the working-age population. This means that an ageing population leads to rising expenditures that cannot be covered without increasing taxes on the young. Politicians have known about population ageing for around 50 years but ignored the problems it will create for public finances.
- Figures for accumulated debt are backward looking, reflecting past deficits; they do not take into account

the promises that governments have made in relation to future commitments. No private sector firm would be able to present accounts in this way.

- If we include commitments that have been made under Social Security and health-care programmes, the US fiscal imbalance is 9 per cent of the estimated present value of future US GDP. This means that an additional 9 per cent of GDP in tax revenues, over and above existing taxes, would have to be levied each year to ensure that all US government spending commitments could be met from taxation. Closing the fiscal gap between expected tax revenues and spending would involve more than doubling federal payroll taxes, assuming that such a rise is economically feasible.

- Under the most realistic assumptions regarding future policy, the US fiscal imbalance is about seven times the total national debt held by the public. In other words, if current unfunded spending commitments to future generations of older people are included, the underlying national indebtedness of the US government is seven times the published figure.

- Over two-thirds of government spending commitments not covered by current tax plans is attributable to two major programmes: Social Security and Medicare. These programmes have been hugely expanded in recent years.

- All the fiscal metrics used by EU countries, for example, in the euro zone's stability and growth pact, are backward-looking measures of accumulated debt;

as such, published debt measures understate true indebtedness.

- The underlying fiscal situation in the EU is worse than that in the US. In EU countries, the ratio of workers to retirees currently stands at between three and four but, for most EU countries, this ratio is projected to decline to below two workers per retiree by the middle of this century. The ratio of workers to retirees will also decline for the US, but will remain considerably above the ratios in the major EU nations.

- This demographic situation, combined with future pension and health-care commitments, is at the heart of the unsustainable budget positions in the EU. The use of explicit debt measures to judge policy leads to bad long-term decision making, especially in areas such as pension provision. For example, in the UK, Poland and Hungary, action has been taken to reduce short-term debt measures in ways that increase long-term state pension liabilities.

- The average fiscal imbalance in the EU is 13.5 per cent of the present value of GDP. Ireland has the highest fiscal imbalance; at 13.6 per cent, the UK's fiscal imbalance is a little above the EU average; and four countries (Sweden, Cyprus, Luxembourg and Estonia) have fiscal imbalances less than 8 per cent.

- A 13.5 per cent fiscal imbalance as a share of GDP in EU nations translates, on average, into a 23.2 percentage point increase in the consumption tax rate if taxes are going to fully finance spending – again assuming that such a rise is feasible. Alternatively, the fiscal imbalance could be closed by reducing health and social protection expenditure by about one half.

- In the UK, total spending would have to be cut by more than one quarter or health and social protection expenditure by around one half compared with the level implied by current policy if the UK is to avoid tax increases and all spending is to be met out of tax revenue in the long run. Some measures have been planned in the UK which will address the situation, such as a proposed rise in state pension age, but these measures are being implemented slowly and are inadequate on their own.

- Faster economic growth than already incorporated into fiscal imbalance estimates is unlikely to resolve governments' long-term fiscal problems. Many of the projected expenditures could increase if there is economic growth because the commitments on pension and health benefits are designed to keep pace with overall economic growth. Furthermore, if countries do not address their fiscal imbalances now, the size of the necessary adjustment will increase over time, undermining investor confidence and generally worsening the conditions for maintaining economic growth. Instead, appropriate and timely structural changes to bring the finances of public programmes into balance would be likely to spur economic growth.

TABLES AND FIGURES

1 INTRODUCTION

Why we need forward-looking measures of government finances

The government's official budget accounts in most developed countries are constructed almost exclusively in terms of current cash flows – mainly government spending and receipts from taxes. In some countries there are exceptions to this. For example, in the US, official budget figures also account for the accrued values of government employee pensions and obligations from past contractual agreements for construction, defence procurement and the like. However, in many other countries – including the UK – even these items are excluded from the headline government debt numbers. As such, the government's borrowing requirement is mostly made up of the difference between current cash inflows and outgoings, although adjustments are sometimes made depending on the debt financing mechanisms in place in the country concerned. A country's national debt is, in effect, the accumulation of all the historical budget deficits. It is therefore almost entirely a backward-looking measure and does not take any account of several major future unfunded payment commitments that modern welfare states make to a country's citizens.

Sometimes it is argued that a government does not need to account for its future financial commitments because it has the power to tax future citizens to meet them, whereas limited liability companies, for example, do not have the power to extract additional funds from their investors. However, this does not mean that it is not important to have measures of a government's financial situation that look forward and demonstrate the level of future spending commitments that cannot be funded by taxes under current policies. After all, it may not be possible for a government to meet its future spending commitments if taxes cannot be raised sufficiently to meet them. Electors, and those who inform them, need to know this. They need to know whether a government can meet all of its future commitments and, if not, what policy actions could be taken. Such policy action would normally involve some combination of reneging on explicit debt, reneging on expenditure commitments to pay social benefits, provide health care and so on, and raising taxes. It is worth noting that particular substantial commitments (such as general retiree pensions and health benefits) may be politically very difficult to roll back. The public needs to know about these policy choices.

International policies that use measures of indebtedness also use backward-looking measures. The European Stability and Growth pact, for example, judges the fiscal probity of a country according to its cash-flow deficit and accumulated historical debt. Future spending commitments are not taken into account at all.

The inter-generational tensions

Comprehensive measurement of a government's long-term fiscal condition began more than two decades ago. The practical measurement of the fiscal condition, especially in the United States and Europe, followed the theoretical work of Martin Feldstein and others, who pointed out that pay-as-you-go public pension and health programmes usually cause substantial wealth redistributions across generations (see Feldstein 1974). Those redistributions occur because the first generation to retire receives windfall benefits despite not having had a history of Social Security or national insurance tax payments when working. Future generations then have benefits promised to them which will be financed by the taxes of still later generations. As the demography of a country changes, the obligations to the older generations can become greater than the taxes that will be levied on future working generations unless there are increases in tax rates.

Redistribution between generations also occurs because the provision of social insurance benefits such as pensions and health services to retired generations induces earlier retirement and higher consumption, which reduces national output, saving and bequests to younger generations (see Auerbach et al. 2001). Consumption is encouraged because it is not necessary for people to save to meet future pensions and health costs and insure against unexpected longevity. Earlier retirement is also encouraged because the individual does not incur the full cost of retiring earlier. The ancillary negative effects on capital formation, labour productivity and inheritances can therefore further impoverish younger and future generations.

These inter-generational economic effects of state pay-as-you-go pension and health-care programmes become stronger if retiree pension and health insurance programmes become more generous over time. This has occurred in both the US and Europe since World War II. This period saw frequent increases in pension benefits, the protection of benefits against inflation, the addition of new health and retirement support programmes and their extension to new population groups among older individuals, their dependants and survivors. The pattern is different in different countries but the general tenor of developments has been the same. Developed countries also experienced an almost two-decade-long baby-boom followed by a 'baby-bust' during the immediate postwar period, creating a large age cohort (the 'boomers') that is now approaching and entering retirement. With significantly faster growth of retiree cohorts compared with younger workers, these countries are now facing significant resource shortfalls when trying to maintain current pension and health commitments to retirees. Meeting the payment obligations will require much higher and economically debilitating taxes on younger generations.

Government-induced wealth redistributions between the generations are also implicit in other government tax and spending programmes. For example, switching taxes from wages to consumption, as has happened in many countries, in a revenue-neutral manner redistributes resources from older to younger generations. The deferment of tax payments by younger generations creates a wealth windfall, whereas the imposition of additional taxes on older generations' consumption leads to a loss.[1] Another example is the recent introduction of Obamacare in the United States, where younger, healthier persons are being forced to purchase health insurance at actuarially unfair annual premiums so that health insurance coverage can be extended at lower than actuarially fair premiums to older and sicker, but hitherto uninsured, individuals. Decisions on whether to increase spending on (for example) education, provide tax relief on mortgages, and so on, also have distributional implications across generations. However, many such policies, especially pay-as-you-go pension and health obligations, are difficult to reverse because a promise has been made to future recipients of the benefit who may well choose, as a result, not to make any provision from their own resources.

The extent of government indebtedness

How large are ongoing wealth redistributions and how would they change if and when the government engages in policy reforms? Making such estimates is not without pitfalls, but approximations can be obtained by combining micro-data survey information with official budget projections to estimate lifetime taxes, transfers and public

---

1 Such a switch in tax bases would also be manifested in a quick devaluation of the capital stock owned by older generations, which younger generations would be able to purchase at lower real prices (see Auerbach and Kotlikoff 1987).

benefits for different birth (or age) cohorts. Such a reorganisation of government budget information can be used to construct fiscal and generational imbalance metrics and generational accounts, which indicate the magnitudes involved.[2] This research monograph reports fiscal imbalances for the US and Europe calculated using official government projections of budget aggregates and micro-data survey information on how those tax and spending items are distributed across the population by age and gender.

The monograph begins by sketching out the fiscal environment in the US and Europe. The concept of inter-generational accounting is then introduced and explained. After examining and quantifying the long-term fiscal problems of the US and the contribution of recent expansions of Medicare to the fiscal imbalances, alternative policy responses are examined and the current US budget debate discussed in the context of the likely implications for future generations. After discussing the policy choices faced by the US, there is then an examination of the long-term fiscal situation in European Union countries.

For the United States, this monograph reports fiscal and generational imbalance measures and generational accounts based on the Congressional Budget Office's (CBO) March 2012 Budget Outlook Update. It finds that the fiscal imbalance embedded in the federal government's current law or baseline policies amounts to 5.4 per cent of the present value of future US GDP, or 11.7 per cent of the present value of future payrolls. However, in the past,

---

2   See Auerbach et al. (1991) and Gokhale and Smetters (2003).

the US government has tended to follow a less fiscally prudent pathway than that which is planned or required by existing law, for example, by not reducing spending or ending tax exemptions. For this reason, the CBO presents a more realistic alternative fiscal scenario. This suggests a federal fiscal imbalance of 9.0 per cent of the present value of all future US GDP or 19.7 per cent of the present value of US payrolls. The US fiscal imbalance is about seven times the total national debt held by the public. In other words, if current unfunded spending commitments to future generations of older people are included, the underlying national indebtedness of the US government is seven times the published figure – hence the title of this monograph, only about one seventh of the US government debt is visible to the electorate.

Measurements of fiscal imbalances are also provided for 25 European Union countries. The average fiscal imbalance in the EU is 13.5 per cent of the present value of GDP. The UK's fiscal imbalance stands at 13.6 percent, which is slightly above the EU average. Four countries – Sweden, Cyprus, Luxembourg and Estonia – have fiscal imbalances less than 8 per cent. The average fiscal imbalance in the EU translates into a 23.2 percentage point increase in the consumption tax rate if taxes are going to fully finance spending, assuming that such a rise is feasible. Alternatively, the fiscal imbalance could be closed by reducing health and social protection expenditure by about 50 per cent. In the UK, total spending would have to be cut by more than one quarter, or health and social protection expenditure by around one half compared with the level implied by current policy if all future spending is to be met through taxation under current policies. The earlier that the US and EU governments implement corrective budget policies, the better will the affected generations be able to prepare for their future economic needs and security.

It is often suggested that countries can inflate their way out of these problems. This is unlikely. Future pay-as-you-go social insurance obligations are generally price index-linked (at least) and health care involves the provision of a set of services. It is unlikely that countries will be able to grow their way out of their implicit debts either. Instead, countries will need to rein in their spending commitments and programmes if they are to avoid huge increases in taxes. Indeed, prior action to reduce unfunded – and likely unpayable – government social spending commitments may be an important precondition for improving policy stability and credibility, reigniting market confidence and triggering faster rates of sustainable economic growth. As a precursor to this, government accounting for future social insurance obligations needs to be undertaken in a much more transparent way than currently. This monograph shows how this can be done. It also indicates the policy choices that will face governments over the difficult decades ahead for public finances across the developed world.

2 THE FISCAL ENVIRONMENT IN EUROPE AND THE UNITED STATES

Europe and the United States will soon begin to encounter fiscal constraints the like of which we have never seen before. In the United States, federal debt as a percentage of GDP has increased rapidly during the last few years, from 57 per cent in 2000 to well over 100 per cent by 2012.[1] According to the US Congressional Budget Office's (CBO) latest long-term projections, total national debt is expected to remain close to 100 per cent of GDP during the next decade and begin to increase thereafter as the baby-boomers fully enter retirement and health and old-age security expenditures outpace federal revenues.[2] Debt levels in European Union countries have surged similarly, from 60 per cent of GDP during the mid 2000s to 85 per cent of GDP

---

1 See the 2013 Economic Report of the President, Government Printing Office of the United States. An alternative US debt measure – debt held by the public as a percentage of GDP – has increased from 35 per cent of national income to 78 per cent during the same period.

2 This conclusion is based on the CBO's 'Updated Budget Projections: Fiscal Years 2013–2023' (May 2013) and the CBO's 'The 2013 Long Term Budget Outlook' (September 2013).

today (see Figures 1 and 2). The upward march of government debt levels has continued unabated during the last decade among major EU nations: by 2012, general government debt had reached 90 per cent of GDP in the United Kingdom and France, 82 per cent in Germany, 84 per cent in Spain, and exceeded well over 100 per cent in Ireland, Greece, Italy and Portugal.[3]

Figure 1 **US federal debt as percentage of GDP**

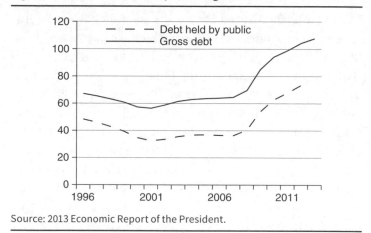

Source: 2013 Economic Report of the President.

Much of the increase in explicit debt in Europe and the United States has been attributed to the Great Recession. Increases in debt-to-GDP ratios were caused by large government stimulus and war spending in the United States as well as a decline followed by a slow recovery in economic growth. In several European Union countries, the debts

---

3   Debt statistics for EU nations are those reported in Eurostat.

built up in private institutions in the banking crisis were assumed by the government through bailouts. Other countries, such as Greece and Italy, faced problems because of profligate public sector spending triggered, at least in part, by easy credit availability in the euro single currency system.

Figure 2 **EU gross debt as percentage of GDP**

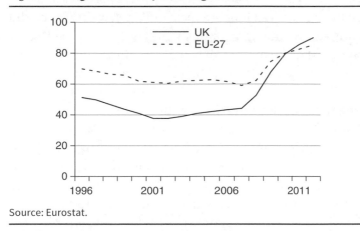

Source: Eurostat.

Restoring both public and private sector debt to lower levels is likely to be a slow process because restoring and recycling impaired bank assets and market confidence takes time. The restoration of private sector financial balance sheets is already underway in the United States. In Europe, stalled discussion about the terms for a new banking union and rules for resolving existing impaired bank balance sheets mean that a similar recovery in the private financial sector may take longer to accomplish. In both regions, however, reducing public sector debt to the pre-2000 level is likely to pose much more serious challenges. That is because explicit debt constitutes only the tip of the 'indebtedness iceberg' that most major EU nations and the United States must resolve. This monograph concerns what lies below sea level when it comes to debt, its measurement and the trade-offs in terms of policy choices involved in resolving the problem. The approach taken in reducing national indebtedness will largely determine the future economic environments in Europe and the United States, that is whether they will remain conducive to output growth and advancing living standards in both regions.

The fiscal background in the euro zone

The EU's fiscal and economic crisis has now lasted for more than three years and does not appear to be nearing a resolution. It has focused policymakers' attention on short-term measures: debt restructuring and bailouts to support fiscally over-extended countries such as Ireland, Portugal, Greece and Spain, and budget consolidations for restoring the short-term solvency of government finances. Most of the focus is on short-term fiscal objectives and measures that are intended to strengthen the European Stability and Growth Pact's criteria and enforcement mechanisms that, so far, have not functioned as expected.

An earlier version of this study of European fiscal imbalances, published in 2009, suggested that European policymakers would find it difficult to navigate the twin transitions of monetary union and demographic change, each placing opposing pressures on national fiscal policies.[4] Successful operation of a monetary union requires consistent and uniform maintenance of stable and sustainable fiscal policies in order to maintain a stable value of the euro by reducing pressure on the European Central Bank (ECB) to monetise government debt. However, population ageing and the increasing globalisation of supply chains are likely to increase social protection demands by retirees and low-skilled workers while international tax competition constrains the raising of taxes for funding those expenditures: this boosts pressure to deficit-finance social protection expenditures. These opposing economic incentives that European policymakers are facing were magnified by the 2008–9 recession, whose effects are still being felt across the continent.

During its early days, the monetary union ensured that all euro zone governments could borrow at similar low interest rates regardless of their current fiscal position and longer-term fiscal condition. The resulting temptation to borrow and spend was reinforced by the asymmetric external and domestic effects that deficit-financed spending exerts, with direct benefits mostly accruing domestically but indirect costs through increased interest rates being distributed across all euro zone member nations. The precise distribution of these costs would depend on the credibility of the euro zone's 'no-bail-out' promise but, in

---

4   See 'Measuring the Unfunded Obligations of European Countries', National Center for Policy Analysis, Policy Report 319, January 2009.

reality, heavily indebted countries were able to borrow at low rates of interest until the crisis hit.

In the aftermath of the recession of 2008–9 and with the currency-devaluation option foreclosed, less competitive EU nations tried to deficit-finance economic stimulus programmes to combat a persistently recessionary environment; there were also costs assumed by governments in respect of bank bailouts while tax revenues fell because of the recession. Fiscal deficits surged in the peripheral countries of Greece and Ireland, increased significantly in Portugal and Spain, and debt levels spiked during 2008–10 in EU nations generally. Reduced investor confidence in public debt management has provoked capital outflows from several euro zone nations (for example, Greece, Portugal, Spain and Italy) and spikes in interest rates raised debt rollover costs and forced yet more public borrowing. Ballooning public debt and capital shortages have also triggered ratings downgrades, compounding the difficulty of reducing public debt levels. Now, repairing housing and financial sectors and restoring market confidence in public debt management to stimulate private investment is likely to be a long and difficult process.[5] With the currency

---

5 Standard & Poor's cut its US rating to AA+ in August 2011, while Fitch and Moody's maintained a negative rating on US sovereign debt. Following Spain's banking crisis, Fitch downgraded that country's credit rating by three levels in January 2012, and maintained a negative outlook. S&P downgraded France's sovereign debt rating by one notch, to Aa1 from Aaa in November 2012, and Moody's simultaneously issued a negative outlook on that country. Moody's removed the UK's triple-A rating in February 2013. Such downgrades of credit ratings are triggered when debt levels

devaluation option closed, peripheral EU countries are attempting to restore competitiveness through temporary bailouts from the stronger nations and by imposing internal austerity-induced wage-price deflation.

However, none of this addresses the long-term fiscal problems that all euro zone countries are facing. The long-term fiscal picture examined in this study shows that even the economically stronger countries, such as Germany, Finland, the Netherlands and France, are facing tight resource constraints because of their social protection commitments. The magnitude of these commitments relative to government receipts available to finance them is strongly influenced by demographic developments. The major EU countries must deal with these long-term shortfalls through budget consolidations, leaving little room for continued bailouts of weaker EU countries.

Fiscal conditions in United Kingdom

Not being a part of the euro zone, the UK is not involved in negotiations on bailout terms for weaker euro zone countries. Within the EU, however, the United Kingdom must consider its options on banking, trade, immigration and fiscal policy harmonisation. Like many other EU nations, the UK is also facing a mountain of explicit and implicit government indebtedness. The UK government deficit surged during the recession,

---

become excessively high, but they compound government financing problems by increasing market interest rates and making debt rollovers more expensive.

reaching 6.9 per cent of GDP during 2008–9 and 11.2 per cent of GDP during 2009–10. Believing, initially, that aggregate demand should be sustained to avoid an even deeper recession, the UK government continued increasing discretionary spending during the recession years of 2008–10. Declining tax revenues and increases in Social Security payments also contributed significantly to the higher deficits during those years. The deficit fell to 9.6 per cent during 2010–11 and 8.0 per cent during 2011–12 and continues to fall somewhat as a proportion of GDP. As a result of this experience, the UK debt-to-GDP ratio stood at 68.5 per cent in November 2012.

Like other EU nations, the UK has also attempted a fiscal consolidation package to limit the explosion in debt. Public spending cutbacks have been focused on areas away from pensions, health and other social protection programmes. Recently announced plans in the UK seek to reduce public spending in 2015 and beyond by 2.7 per cent over spending originally projected for 2014, with the spending reductions being focused on areas such as the judicial, community and local government sectors. Notwithstanding concerns that austerity budget measures (that mostly target public non-social-protection spending) cannot repair debt-to-GDP levels because they would only slow GDP growth, budget cutbacks are expected to set the conditions for renewed growth through private investment as market confidence in the sustainability and stability of budget policies improves. The question remains about whether this policy can succeed without paring expenditure commitments on health, social protection and state pensions.

The UK's longer-term outlook does have a positive aspect that is not shared by many other EU countries: a more robust population increase from a resurgent birth rate. Annual UK births since mid year 2011 have registered their highest level since 1972. Sustaining the recent uptick in UK births would ease deficit and debt pressures in the long term if the general government policy environment supports investment in human and physical capital. Insofar as this requires higher government spending, it would be better to finance it through expenditure reductions in other budget sectors rather than through higher taxes.

Fiscal conditions in the United States

In the United States, the official (gross) federal debt of $17 trillion includes only outstanding US Treasury securities on which contractual future payments are due. Of this, about $12 trillion is held by the public (including foreign holders and financial institutions), the rest being held in US agency accounts representing investment of past agency surpluses such as the US Social Security programme (see Figure 1). At the time of writing, the Congressional Budget Office projects US debt held by the public to increase to $19 trillion and gross federal debt (which includes debt held in government accounts) to exceed $25 trillion by 2023.[6]

---

6 Projections taken from the CBO's May 2013 Budget and Economic Outlook update, and from the President's budget for fiscal year 2014, published in April 2013, United States Government Printing Office.

There are two caveats to the projections cited above. Firstly, the US federal government has one set of policies on the books but appears to be following a different set. The government alters fiscal policies in ways that will decrease financial burdens on specific voter segments (either through lower taxes or through increased expenditures). One example of this is the frequent postponement of cuts to doctors' Medicare reimbursements to prevent their exodus from the Medicare system. Another is the frequent adjustments to the tax brackets of the Alternative Minimum Tax (AMT) that subjects those with high incomes to additional taxes. This is done to prevent current-law AMT rules drawing in middle-income taxpayers. Frequent adjustments of this type means that today's generations are required to pay less in taxes or they receive more in transfers or compensation for services. But, given the spending trajectory of the rest of government on public goods and services provision, those financial 'giveaways' to current generations must eventually be paid for by future ones through higher taxes or reduced transfers.

Secondly, the official explicit debt reflects only a part of the government's indebtedness because the government 'owes' future payments to millions of additional individuals – those who will become eligible for Social Security pensions, Medicare, unemployment, disability, food stamps and other government entitlement and welfare programmes as well as those who will provide defence, infrastructure, education and other public services. The government also 'forgoes' tax collections from millions of others through tax exemption and preference programmes: for example, those with children, for business expenses, those with low earnings and participants in qualifying retirement saving programmes. European national governments also have similar obligations – to pay citizens benefits and provide public services – that must be paid for out of future revenues. In almost all Western developed nations, revenues projected under current policies are smaller than the government obligations under existing programmes, implying much larger public sector indebtedness than the explicit debt numbers inherited from past budget outcomes convey.

Indeed, in both Europe and the United States, benefits under social security programmes may be more firmly entrenched than contractual payments on sovereign bonds. In the United States, for example, entitlement programme beneficiaries who paid payroll taxes while working feel a strong moral and legal entitlement to retirement, survivor, health and other benefits and they possess growing political clout to maintain those benefits as 'promised'. In some countries, some of the future government obligations are contractual, such as pensions to be paid to public sector employees. Indeed, the inviolate nature of US Social Security and Medicare obligations may exceed that of federal bond liabilities because, unlike most US government bonds, entitlements are universally protected against inflation. In Europe as well, public sector unions and other political pressure groups work strenuously to protect their constituents' public benefits.

If by general consensus the benefits of social security programmes are considered sacrosanct, the unfunded components of such obligations – those exceeding projected government revenues – should be included in national debt measures. Indeed, going further and including the unfunded components of all government programmes in indebtedness measures seems warranted but they are not included in official government budget reports.[7] This monograph calculates and reports more inclusive and comprehensive measures of national indebtedness which do take account of government promises. It shows that the true degree of indebtedness with which policymakers must contend is much larger across most EU nations and the United States than the official debt figures.

Population ageing in Europe and the United States

One obvious contributor to high public-sector indebtedness in the US and EU is ongoing population ageing in both regions. Age–dependency ratios in both regions are projected to continue increasing from today through the mid 2030s and beyond.[8] As Figure 3 shows, this ratio is projected to remain smaller for the United States than

---

7   The $17 trillion official figure of US explicit gross debt only includes the contractual debt of the Treasury to the Social Security and Medicare trust funds – equal to the accumulated value of past payroll tax surpluses. But those trust funds fall woefully short of the total unfunded future payment obligations that Social Security and Medicare are facing.

8   The age–dependency ratio is calculated by dividing the populations aged 65 and older by the population aged 15–64 in each of the years shown in Figure 3.

for the EU-27 region, reflecting a historically higher fertility-plus-net-immigration rate. In turn, the projected increase in the UK's age–dependency ratio is less rapid than in the EU-27 region as a whole because of the UK's higher projected fertility-plus-immigration rates. In the EU-27 region, the age–dependency ratio is projected to continue increasing well into the 2050s if today's very low fertility rates (which are below the replacement rate) persist into the future.

Figure 3   **Age dependency ratios in the EU, the UK and the US**

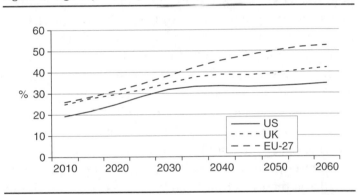

An ageing population alone does not create greater national indebtedness unless combined with social security programmes that are mostly funded concurrently out of payroll and other taxes generally levied on the working-age population. One way to ensure adequate funding for future needs is through setting aside sufficient funds during workers' careers to cover their consumption, health and other spending needs during old age as would generally happen in a privately funded pension arrangement. However, given that most social protection and safety net programmes are operated on a pay-as-you-go basis in both the US and the EU, an ageing population portends rising expenditures that cannot be covered without increasing taxes on the young if benefit levels are to be sustained at levels required by current laws.

The fact of population ageing has been known for a long time – for at least 50 years – since the post-war surge in fertility rates was fully reversed by the mid 1960s. But policymakers continued to expand existing social security and safety net programmes and established new ones to transfer yet more resources from workers to retirees. Indeed, the extension in 2003 by the US government of new Medicare prescription drug coverage for retirees was enacted without any explicit or dedicated funding provision. Policymakers preferred to ignore the fact that the demographic bulge and continued population ageing from increasing longevity would create a massive debt overhang. The size of such public sector indebtedness is not computed and reported by official budget scoring agencies in the US and rarely in other countries. This is a situation that policymakers appear to comprehend but allow to persist.

All of this raises fundamental questions about why we lack farsighted policymakers informed by an appropriately long-range fiscal vocabulary and policy relevant metrics. At root, however, the reason that we now have a Damoclean sword of high and rising indebtedness hanging over us is because of the quick and easy willingness of past generations of policymakers to exploit the 'fiscal commons' of future resources and productivity. The fiscal innovations that enabled such borrowing from the future became progressively more popular in the developed world after the advent during the 1930s of pay-as-you-go financed social security programmes.

Government off-balance-sheet borrowing

Most governments in the developed world use systems of budgeting based on cash-flow accounting. Such a system tracks the government's net monetary inflow – roughly equal to the annual surplus or deficit – and records the evolution of debt metrics such as gross national debt and debt held by the public (excluding intra-governmental debt from gross national debt). Such a cash-flow accounting system may be appropriate for daily management of the budget, but it is inadequate for informing policy-makers about the choices they face in a way that would ease their evaluation and understanding of the trade-offs involved. For example, a commitment by government to spend £100m extra on teachers' salaries would, all else equal, increase government borrowing in the relevant year by £100m. However, a contractual commitment in the same year to increase teachers' future pensions by £100m in present value would not alter the current year's budget deficit even though this obligation is just as large and just as binding.[9] Both these promises have the same impact on

---

9   Interestingly, given the design of most government worker pension schemes, the salary increase would also lead to an increase in

future taxpayers. In the first case, the government will borrow £100m and future taxpayers will have to service the debt. In the second case, future taxpayers will have to pay additional pension costs. However, the first policy option appears to cost £100m whereas the second policy option appears to cost nothing under standard cash-flow deficit and debt metrics. Such an approach to accounting would be totally unacceptable in the private sector. The method of accounting used in the public sector obscures or misrepresents the cost of different policy options and is therefore likely to lead to poor policy choices at the expense of future generations.

Attempts to enact balanced budget amendments to the US Constitution suggest that many observers and policymakers think that such a constraint would deliver the correct policies on average. They also suggest that voters are concerned about government indebtedness. Various attempts have been made to restrain governments' current spending to the level of their current income in a number of European countries as well. But what constitutes a balanced budget? In common parlance, it is associated with a zero fiscal deficit summing across all government programmes and operations (often called zero unified budget deficits).

Several arguments are usually proffered in support of targeting zero budget deficits overall (although some economists suggest that this objective is appropriate only for

---

future pensions obligations, a fact that is almost entirely ignored in the standard approaches to government accounting.

the government's 'non-investment' outlays). These arguments include the following:

- All taxpayer cohorts should 'pay their own way' whereas cash-flow deficits push tax burdens onto future taxpayers.
- Deficits divert investible resources from private investment towards government consumption.
- High debt implies that interest outlays capture a large share of government revenues that could otherwise be allocated to productive uses.
- Under the current system of government, explicit rules are needed to limit the government's ability to run large deficits.

Irrespective of their validity, these arguments suggest that attempts to improve the budget process mostly focus on eliminating cash-flow deficits. This means equating annual revenues to annual outlays, on average. Zero deficits would be achieved if programmes with earmarked revenues were financed on a pay-as-you-go basis and the government's discretionary spending were maintained below general tax revenues net of interest outlays. In other words, cash-flow accounting and targeting zero deficits creates a bias towards adopting pay-as-you-go financing, especially if the population is likely to age so that current costs of pay-as-you-go benefits can easily be met from current taxes, even though the situation may reverse in the future. This is true for individual programmes, such as health and pension systems, and for the budget as a whole.

Unfortunately, pay-as-you-go financing of social security systems involves sizeable redistributions of fiscal burdens (that is, tax payments net of transfer receipts) across the generations. Those costs will be borne by those who cannot yet vote and, indeed, have not yet been born. These policies often erode work incentives – because of the redistribution and higher taxes that are involved – and reduce saving and capital formation because those who benefit from pay-as-you-go programmes generally consume at a higher rate.

Understanding the inter-generational transfers

How pay-as-you-go financed programmes – such as state pensions systems in most of the developed world – transfer resources from younger and future generations to those alive today can be understood through Figure 4.

The horizontal axis shows time in years beginning from the current year (period 0). The vertical axis shows age ranging from 0 (for newborns) to 90 – for the purposes of illustration an assumed maximum age of the human lifetime. The dark shaded squares trace the prospective life trajectory of this year's newborns. In 20 years' time they will be aged 20, in 64 years' time they will be aged 64, and so on.

In period 0, the population distribution by age is situated in the cells in the first *y*-axis column (vertically above the *x*-axis square marked with a '0'). For example, the light-grey square represents those aged 20 in period 0. The prospective life trajectory of each generation alive today would be traced by the 45° line of cells beginning with the corresponding age cell in period 0. For example,

Figure 4 **Inter-generational transfers in pay-as-you-go systems**

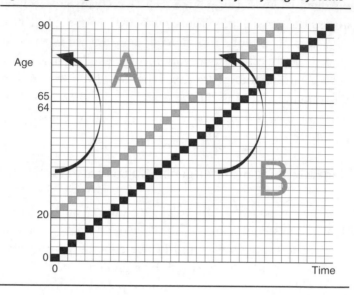

the light-grey cells show the prospective life trajectory of those who are 20 years old today – at time 1 such a person would be 21, and so on. The black-shaded life trajectory of today's newborns separates current generations' lifetimes (the triangular area of the graph above this trajectory marked as region 'A') from those of future ones – those not yet born as of period 0 (marked as region 'B'). For example, the diagonal line of squares immediately above the black line shows the trajectory of a one-year-old (he will be two in one year's time, and so on); however, the diagonal line immediately below the black line shows the life trajectory of somebody who will be born in one year (he will be born next year and will be one in two years' time, and so on).

Assume that the government establishes a pay-as-you-go financed social security programme in period 0. This programme imposes a payroll tax on those aged 20–64 inclusive and pays out all the resulting revenues as old-age benefits to retirees aged 65 and older. This transfer is indicated by the curved arrow – shifting resources from those aged 20–64 in period 0 to those aged 65+ in period 0. The new social security programme is to be permanent, promising social security benefits to retirees in each future period financed from the new payroll tax levied on workers. Because the revenue increase under the new programme is identical to the increase in benefit expenditures, this is a strictly deficit neutral (i.e. pay-as-you-go) programme. Although the total amount of the economy's resources redirected by the government increases from adopting such a programme, the annual deficit or surplus – the government's net cash flow – does not change, by construction.

Because the new programme is permanent, however, it will initiate 'valid expectations' on the part of current workers of receiving benefits in the future in exchange for their current payroll taxes. But who will fund those future benefits? It will be future workers, including those not born as of period 0, when the programme was established. In Figure 4 the curved arrow on the right-hand side shows future transfers from workers belonging to current and future-born generations (as of period 0) to future retirees. Unlike the curved arrow on the left, this arrow crosses the dark-shaded life trajectory of today's newborns, indicating a redistribution of resources from future generations (region B) to those alive today (region A). Such redistribution

– from younger and future generations towards older ones alive today – is accomplished by establishing a new pay-as-you-go financed social security programme without ever incurring cash-flow budget deficits. Thus, pay-as-you-go programmes (and deficit-neutral expansions of such programmes) increase the resources of those alive today at the expense of those who will be alive in the future.

Can we afford pay-as-you-go programmes because our children will be richer?

Some policymakers and practitioners argue that resource redistributions from future to current generations are justified because the former will be more prosperous, partly because of the latter's prior productive innovations and investment. This reasoning rings true and is the basis for supporting the debt financing of those public investments that have an acceptable rate of return. Unfortunately, drawing a clear line between consumption and investment goods purchases by the government is extremely difficult. Furthermore, pay-as-you-go pension systems do not facilitate any such investment (indeed, arguably, they appear more likely to reduce the types of private sector saving and investment that might make future generations richer). There are also no fiscal metrics or budget processes to effectively constrain the extent of inter-generational redistributions in pay-as-you-go pension systems. How would we know when we have gone too far? What would happen if the increase in obligations to pay pensions imposed upon future generations far outpaces those which can be afforded by increases in productivity? Needless to say, these issues are worth debating in greater detail but such discussions should be informed by clear metrics about the size of ongoing inter-generational redistributions.

Of course, the real difficulties arise when one or more of three problems manifest themselves. Firstly, sustained productivity growth that initiators of such pay-as-you-go programmes usually cite as a justification for adopting them does not occur. Secondly, the number of children who are born is insufficient to sustain the balance between pay-as-you-go spending and revenues. Thirdly, transfers to retirees are larger because people live longer than expected. These factors may lead to the total amount of required transfers increasing and/or the total amount of taxes available to finance the transfers at current tax rates falling (because there are fewer younger people or there is slower economic growth). Calculating government budgets under a cash-flow accounting system is inadequate for evaluating potentially large resource redistributions from future generations (region B in Figure 4).

Algebraic presentation of inter-generational accounting

Assuming unchanged fiscal policies, the government's future expenditure obligations for purchasing public goods and services – such as defence, infrastructure, foreign diplomacy, judicial services, etc. (P) – must be paid for out of the sum of (1) the government's net financial wealth (NFW), (2) net tax payments by current generations (NTC), and (3) net tax payments by future generations (NTF). Thus, we can express the government's inter-temporal budget identity (under current fiscal policies) as

$$P^c = NFW + NTC^c + NTF. \tag{1}$$

In this identity, the superscript 'c' indicates the assumption that projections of government purchases and current generations' net tax payments are made under current fiscal policies. The expressions for net tax payments, NTC and NTF, are net of any benefits received by the relevant generation, such as social security or health-care costs, current or future respectively.

This identity can be the basis for constructing an alternative set of forward-oriented fiscal metrics to reflect the full scope of the inter-generational resource redistribution being implemented under current fiscal policies. The item P is the present discounted value of projected government purchase of public goods and services. NFW can be obtained from the government's financial accounts as the accumulated value of past government budget surpluses. NFW is usually a negative item as most Western developed governments have consistently incurred budget deficits in the past. For example, the US government's NFW equals explicit debt held by the public of $12 trillion.

We can estimate NTC^c by allocating aggregate officially projected taxes and transfers by age and gender using micro-data information on those payments and receipts by various age and gender cohorts and assuming that those per-capita amounts would grow over time at the economy's average (projected) rate of productivity growth.

These projected future per-capita net tax payments (tax payments minus transfer receipts) can be summed and discounted over the future populations and life trajectories of those alive today (corresponding to region A in Figure 4) to yield NTC^c.

Calculating $P^c - NFW - NTC^c$, with each item evaluated under current policies, shows the total resources that must be raised in present value terms as net tax payments from future generations (NTF) to balance (or 'close') the government's inter-temporal budget.

Note that policies that transfer resources from future generations towards current generations reduce NTC^c and, given P^c, directly imply a higher required value of NTF. Thus, re-estimating NTC under a different set of fiscal policies (say, after the introduction of a new pay-as-you-go social security programme) and recalculating NTF (as $P^c - NFW - NTC^c$) would capture the shift in fiscal burdens from today's to future generations – that is, the extent to which the new policy raids the future 'fiscal commons'.

Note that under the calculation method described above for identity (1), only current generations' fiscal treatment is maintained under current fiscal policies. Future generations are assumed to pick up the residual fiscal (net tax) burden whatever it turns out to be. Alternatively, we could also project the net tax payment by future generations under current fiscal laws and practices and calculate the fiscal imbalance (FI^c):

$$FI^c = P^c - NFW - NTC^c - NTF^c. \qquad (2)$$

This alternative approach does not assume that the budget gap is 'closed' by increasing the tax burden or reducing transfers to the next generation. Instead, FI^c shows the unfunded portion of the government's spending obligations under the assumption that current fiscal laws and practices will be maintained for all current and future generations.

For transfer programmes with dedicated funding, the term $-(NFW + NTC^c)$ indicates the excess transfer payments being awarded to past and current generations under the programme's current policies. Because the terms are defined as the net taxes paid after deducting the benefits received, it is the negative of the sum of these terms that defines the excess transfer payments. This metric $-(NFW + NTC^c)$ is called the 'closed group' unfunded obligation (or 'generational imbalance', GI^c) because it covers only past and current generations but excludes future ones.[1] As discussed in more detail below, the generational imbalance metric, GI^c, is a useful complement to the FI^c metric because it shows the portion of the latter that is accounted for by past and current generations.

---

1   The generational imbalance measure $-(NTC + NFW)$ shows the excess of prospective transfer payments to current generations over their prospective taxes (recall that NTC records taxes minus transfers). Subtracting the programme's financial assets accumulated in the past shows the total fiscal cost that the programme would eventually transfer to future generations (region B of Figure 4) if the programme's current tax and transfer policies are maintained. Of course, this could be negative.

Why calculate fiscal and generational imbalances?

The purpose of calculating fiscal imbalance metrics is twofold. Firstly, they help demonstrate whether current policies are sustainable in the long term or whether they will have to be changed at some point in the future. Many individuals have criticised inter-generational measures of fiscal policy as being based on a future economic and fiscal environment (the continuation of current fiscal policies) that will not actually happen. Indeed, this criticism is true, but misses the point. We require the fiscal imbalance measures under current policies and practices precisely to characterise those policies, to indicate to policymakers whether those policies should be changed and to provide metrics that reveal the trade-offs in terms of which generations would be affected under alternative future policy options.

A large FI^c (fiscal imbalance) cannot be continued indefinitely because it will grow larger through the accumulation of interest costs, eventually triggering the loss of market confidence, spikes in interest rates and a government funding crisis. Such a crisis will trigger policy changes, providing credence to the critics that the assumptions underlying the calculation of the FI^c metric are very unlikely to be sustained. By definition, then, if the assumption that current fiscal laws and practices would continue indefinitely reveals a large FI^c, that result itself reveals the impossibility of sustaining those policies and practices. The FI^c metric, therefore, only characterises the cost and sustainability of current fiscal laws and practices and is not intended as a forecast of future policies or the future economic environment. In the same way as somebody with a satellite navigation system might set it to provide information about a journey time on a highly congested route and then use that information to change route, the fiscal course can be changed if we know the cost – in advance – of not changing course.

The advantage of calculating the FI^c embedded in a given set of government policies and practices flows from the ability of this metric to reveal how far policies must be changed to eliminate the imbalance. There are two possible intuitive explanations for a fiscal imbalance. Firstly, because it represents the present value shortfall in projected government revenues compared with projected government expenditures, it shows the amount of additional funds that the government must have on hand today to cover those future funding shortfalls. This is the measure that is obtained when the fiscal imbalance is expressed as a present value. Secondly, given that the government does not have such a fund in hand, there must be a policy change at some point in the future to generate the additional resources to plug the estimated resource shortfalls under current policies. This could be done by cutting back spending promises or increasing government tax and other receipts. The FI^c metric can be calculated to indicate the extent to which government policies and practices would have to be changed. If spending policy changes are targeted, we can calculate the size of the future spending cuts that would eliminate the fiscal imbalance. Alternatively, we can calculate the increase in the level of taxes necessary to plug the long-term gap. Of course, there may be a mixture of strategies. If we take the ratio of the fiscal imbalance to the payroll base this shows the average permanent increase in payroll taxes that is necessary to eliminate the fiscal imbalance assuming current spending policies are continued.

For programmes that are funded exclusively from dedicated resources – such as Social Security in the US – calculation of the additional metric of the generational imbalance, GI^c, shows how any adjustments of taxes or transfers (or to other policy levers that indirectly influence them – such as changes in the age from which pension benefits are received) would redistribute the fiscal costs of participating in such programmes. For example, when social security policies are altered, the change in social security's GI^c shows the portion of total change in social security's FI^c that would affect the current generation's cheque books. And the residual ($FI^c - GI^c$) is the portion that would affect future generations' cheque books. Thus, GI^c shows how fiscally responsible a policy change would be that aims to reduce FI^c. For such programmes, the fiscal imbalance metric indicates the size of future revenue shortfalls and the generational imbalance metric shows how the burden of a particular fiscal adjustment would be distributed across today's generation and future generations of participants.

How should fiscal imbalances be reported?

Fiscal and generational imbalances – which are discounted present values of future unfunded government expenditures – can be reported in dollars (or pounds), as a ratio to the present value of future GDP, or as a ratio of the present value of a particular tax (for example, a tax on payrolls or incomes), or as a ratio of some form of government expenditure (for example, general government expenditure, discretionary expenditure, mandatory expenditure, social insurance expenditure). Each alternative way of expressing the fiscal imbalance metric indicates how large the fiscal imbalance is relative to a given base. For example, the calculations reported in this monograph show that the US fiscal imbalance equals 9 per cent of the estimated present value of future US GDP. In other words, one would have to set aside 9 per cent of GDP each year in the future to achieve inter-temporal government budget balance and to ensure that the government can meet all its future spending obligations that are not met out of current tax plans. Alternatively, this equals about 19 per cent of the present value of future payrolls, indicating that an additional tax equal to about 19 per cent would have to be levied, on average, on the earnings of future workers to achieve the same result.[2]

In discussion of government indebtedness and future pension obligations, fiscal imbalances are often described in terms of the proportion of one year's national income. For example, UK government indebtedness might be

---

2   It is worth noting in passing that, though these figures will be discussed in greater detail below, this does not simply mean an increase of 19 per cent in the tax rate as taxes are not levied on all earnings normally.

described as approximately 80 per cent of GDP and unfunded state pension obligations to public sector workers as a figure of similar magnitude. If we sum all the future government unfunded obligations, a sum of around 400 per cent of GDP is frequently quoted. However, this is not the best mechanism for illustrating fiscal imbalances, though it might help in the comparison of different types of obligations or provide a rule of thumb. Fiscal imbalances should be calculated in relation to spending and tax revenue going forward over several generations as future commitments will not be met out of one year's national income. The imbalance should therefore be measured with reference to national income or tax and spending rate changes over the same time horizon.

4 FISCAL POLICY UNDER SHORT-TERM AND LONG-TERM FISCAL METRICS

Short-term fiscal metrics and the distortion of policy

Although appropriate when an economy is in a recession, intensively focusing on short-term objectives may divert policymakers' attention from the fact that longer-term fiscal shortfalls arising from structural budget imbalances must also be addressed. Indeed, such shortfalls, which are large and growing in several EU nations and in the US, would be easier to deal with if action were taken earlier rather than later. Budget crises provide opportunities for tax and spending reforms that address both short-term and long-term imbalances.

But it is not just the fact that most developed economies are currently experiencing slow growth or recessions that generate exclusive focus on short-term budget objectives and policies. Exclusive concentration on short-term objectives is also facilitated by the constant use of short-term and backward-oriented fiscal metrics. As mentioned earlier with respect to policymaking in the US, past experience shows that, once policy targets under those metrics are achieved, policymakers readily abandon the fiscal rules and constraints that improved the short-term budget balance even though maintaining the constraints may be necessary to ensure structural or long-term budget balance.

Only the achievement of long-term budget balance can yield fiscal policy stability – a crucial element of the economic environment that would be conducive to maximising private investment and delivering sustained economic growth and employment.

The US's fiscal policies during the 1990s and early 2000s are a case in point. The Budget Enforcement Act of 1990 – motivated by runaway deficits and debt during the late 1980s – imposed tight constraints on federal spending and introduced restrictions on social protection expenditure increases. Along with the positive impulse to economic growth and government revenues from new technology in the 1990s, this helped to improve the nation's short-term budget balance as measured by cash-flow deficits and the national debt. But the long-term budget outlook remained contingent on maintaining the Budget Enforcement Act's fiscal course. By the early 2000s, however, policymakers' focus on short-term and backward-looking metrics, which deficits and debt represent, created a greater comfort level and politicians seemed happy to spend projected budget surpluses. The urge to spend those surpluses intensified as the George W. Bush Administration assumed control of the US government. The Act was then allowed to expire in 2002 and federal spending on new defence and non-defence items and on discretionary and mandatory social protection initiatives accelerated sharply.[1] Thus, projections by

---

1   Historical data from the Congressional Budget Office show that inflation-adjusted federal non-defence discretionary expenditures *decreased* at an average annual rate of 2.6 per cent per year between 1991 and 2001. After 2002, however, those expenditures

official budget scoring agencies of ten-year budget surpluses under the Budget Enforcement Act proved to be
temporary.[2] The illusion created by focusing on cash-flow
debts and deficits that the nation's fiscal problems had
been solved induced US politicians to commence a phase
of grandiose fiscal munificence toward their constituents.
As the new round of tax cuts, spending increases, entitlement expansions and war expenditures began, the long-
term – and now even the near-term – US fiscal outlook has
worsened considerably.[3]

The basic problem is the same as that which would arise
in any entity that accounted on a cash-flow basis. If an

---

increased at an average annual rate of 6.1 per cent through 2011.
Inflation-adjusted defence discretionary expenditures grew at an
average annual rate of 2.1 per cent between 1991 and 2001; post-
2002 they grew at an average annual rate of 4 per cent.

2   Congressional Budget Office (CBO), 'The Economic and Budget
Outlook: An Update', 1 July 1999. The budget outlook in this report states: 'If current laws and policies remain unchanged and
the economy performs as CBO assumes, the excess of total federal
revenues over total federal outlays will grow from $120 billion in
1999 to $413 billion in 2009, CBO estimates (see Table 5). If those
surpluses are realized, past borrowing from the public will be sub-
stantially repaid, and debt held by the public will fall from $3,720
billion at the end of 1998 to $865 billion at the end of 2009.' Instead,
federal debt at the end of 2009 stood at $7.5 trillion. And the CBO's
most recent Budget and Economic Outlook (from August 2012)
shows that federal debt will reach $11.3 trillion by the end of 2012.

3   The Congressional Budget Office's 'Alternative' federal budget projections show a ten-year cumulative deficit of $9.9 trillion through
to the year 2022. See 'An Update to the Budget and Economic
Outlook: Fiscal Years 2012 to 2022,' United States' Congressional
Budget Office, August 2012.

insurance company believed that it was solvent because the premiums paid by policyholders in a given year were greater than the benefits paid out, while benefit promises for future years were entirely ignored, it would soon become bankrupt – indeed, it would be acting illegally. The short-term fiscal metrics used by government only account for the cash flows that occur in a given year and not the commitments that governments take on for future years in the hope that they can be financed from future taxes. As such, the accounting metrics used by government not only provide misleading information but they also encourage politicians to behave in a way that is not prudent in the long term. We have illustrated how this distortion affects policy in the US, but it is also apparent in many other countries. For example, in the euro zone, the government debt and deficit targets that have been required under the stability and growth pact have been measured purely in terms of current cash accounting with no account taken of future commitments.

Constructing long-term fiscal and generational imbalance measures

The fiscal imbalance metric shows the extra resources that the government would require for covering future shortfalls of revenues under current fiscal laws and practices. The better way of presenting this metric is not in current cash terms but as a ratio of the present value of a country's future GDP (or, alternatively, as a ratio of the present value of future payrolls, or consumption or other tax bases that might be used to finance future obligations). The fiscal imbalance ratio shows the size of the policy change with respect to projected GDP (or, alternatively, the tax base) that would be required to resolve future shortfalls.

The fiscal imbalance ratio metric is computed for the US, where both the fiscal imbalance and the present value of GDP are calculated in perpetuity. This is feasible because underlying assumptions – fertility, mortality and immigration rates by age and gender – are available in sufficient detail to extend the official Social Security Administration population projections for many decades into the future. For European nations, however, the fiscal imbalance ratio metrics presented in later chapters are only calculated through to the year 2060, the last year for which official (Eurostat) population projections are available. An extension of population projections similar to that implemented for the US has proved untenable for EU countries.[4]

Age–gender distributions of budget items in the initial years, beginning in a base year of 2010 for which budget projections are available, are constructed using microdata survey information. Those distributions are then used to extend aggregate budget projections into future years at historically observed or officially assumed productivity growth rates adjusted for inflation. The extended budget

---

4 Using Eurostat's fertility, mortality and immigration assumptions to extend population projections beyond the year 2060 produces a population implosion in some EU nations within a few decades after 2060. This in itself should be worrying and is indicative of major problems that might not be revealed even by the figures in this study.

projections of government receipts, purchases and transfer benefits are discounted using inflation-adjusted interest rates on long-term government bonds. The discounting is implemented back to the base year so that all future cash payments and receipts are placed on a par with the cash-flow values in the base year. The government's existing net worth and the sum across all current and future generations of the present discounted value of their taxes net of transfers (into perpetuity for the US and through to 2060 for EU nations) is subtracted from the present discounted value of government purchases – all calculated under current fiscal laws and practices (as indicated in Equation (2) above). The difference equals the fiscal imbalance or total unfunded obligations of the government that must eventually be eliminated or paid for through future policy changes.[5]

Disaggregating the fiscal imbalance for the US

In many countries, there are dedicated revenues for certain programmes even though it might be possible to use general revenue streams to finance benefits. This is true, for example, in the UK, where national insurance contributions are separate from other general tax revenues but general revenues can be used to pay pensions and unemployment benefits and so on. The availability of detailed

---

5   For EU nations, the fiscal imbalance is reported for the general government, which includes subnational government entities. For the US, however, data availability permitted the calculation only for the federal government.

budget projections from the US Congressional Budget Office, including information on the financing structure of Social Security pensions and Medicare, enables calculation of specific generational imbalance metrics for those two programmes in the US. Unfortunately, all the information necessary to make similar generational imbalance estimates for specific programmes is not available for European countries.

The US Supplementary Medical Insurance (SMI) is one such programme that is partly financed out of dedicated receipts. Its fiscal and generational imbalance calculation reveals the excess of the present value of SMI benefits over dedicated receipts as SMI's imbalance. Any general revenues used to pay for SMI benefits would affect the fiscal imbalance reported in the government's general account: treating SMI's general revenue funding on a par with its dedicated revenues would reduce SMI's fiscal imbalance (to zero) but would correspondingly increase the imbalance in the general government account, leaving the federal government's total fiscal imbalance unchanged. The disaggregation provides additional useful information, but the aggregate figure is more relevant when looking at the government's overall fiscal condition.

The generational imbalance calculations also separate the fiscal imbalance into that part of the fiscal imbalance that is attributable to past and current generations (the generational imbalance) and the remainder of the fiscal imbalance that is attributable to future generations. This is helpful in understanding issues of inter-generational equity and in judging the appropriateness of particular reform programmes as is discussed in the box.

This decomposition also helps to isolate the net excess benefits that past and current generations would receive if current budget policies are left unchanged. Since programmes must eventually be adjusted to reduce the fiscal imbalance to zero, the change in the generational imbalance measure reveals the extent to which those policy adjustments would affect current generations. Thus, a change in the generational imbalance arising from alterations to Social Security pensions and Medicare taxes and expenditures is an indication of how 'fiscally responsible' those policy changes are. If an initially positive generational imbalance declines from adopting a particular set of Social Security pensions and Medicare policy adjustments, it means that the net excess benefits of past and current generations (that they would obtain under those programmes' current fiscal policies) would be smaller under the changed policies. In effect the government would be forcing those generations to pay for more of the benefits that they are to receive from those programmes or would be reducing their benefits to the extent that they are in excess of the taxes that the generation has paid into the programmes in the past.

Thus, the fiscal imbalance metric informs policymakers on the size of the government's total future revenue shortfall (in discounted present value terms) and the generational imbalance measure informs policymakers about the amount of that imbalance arising from excess benefits

Current generations versus future generations: a stylised example

Assume that a government has just embarked on a radical pension and health reform. This reform requires all young people entering the labour market henceforth to save and insure for their pensions and health needs for all their family and does not provide any state support whatsoever under any circumstances. Furthermore, there is no other form of government spending. Assuming that some taxes remain, the value of taxes less spending attributable to future generations will be positive because future generations will pay taxes but not receive social security and health benefits. However, there could still be a fiscal imbalance because of unfunded benefit commitments made to current retirees and those workers who will retire over the coming 30 years or so, especially if tax rates are low.

Policymakers may wish to consider the appropriate policy response in the context of the fiscal imbalance. For example, a rise in taxes on the current middle-aged and older generations might be the fiscally responsible approach (perhaps by increasing consumption taxes relative to taxes on earnings) as it would impose adjustment costs on the beneficiaries of past excess commitments. But this may not be fully appropriate and fair, especially for today's poorer retirees with few or no employment prospects. Alternatively, the government may decide to borrow to pay for the pensions and health care of the current generation and pay that borrowing off through a tax rise just sufficient to service that debt in perpetuity. This policy option would impose some of the adjustment cost on younger and future generations. One policy response that may seem especially inappropriate would be a steep rise in taxes that only affects the very young generations who are also required to pay for their own pensions and health care, followed by a fall in taxes to zero once the obligations to the current older generation have been met. Under this policy, all the adjustment cost would fall on today's youngest generation which will have to fund pensions and health care for itself and its forebears. The actual policies adopted may be more complicated than those described here; for example, a switch in tax base from income and payroll to consumption taxes together with an increase in the retirement age. In such cases, policy evaluation through FI^c and GI^c metrics would correctly reflect how much of the imbalance is being resolved and how the adjustment burden is being shared across today's and future generations.

to past and current generations through their participation in particular social insurance programmes. These two metrics taken together provide a powerful tool for policymakers to select from among the myriad alternative policies that could be adopted to resolve any fiscal imbalance embedded in current fiscal policies.

5 US PUBLIC POLICY DEBATES: CAUGHT IN A PRISONER'S DILEMMA

The US Congressional Budget Office's federal budget projections (2013–22) from March 2012 show that federal outlays on long-term entitlement programmes (such as Social Security pensions, Medicare and Medicaid, and other long-term retirement and health programmes including federal civilian and military retirement and veterans benefit programmes) already constitute 50 per cent of gross federal outlays.[1] The CBO's projections also show that these programmes will take up 67 per cent of the federal budget by the end of its ten-year budget window.[2] And given that population ageing will continue well beyond 2022, these programmes' budget share is expected to grow even larger during the coming decades.

The growth of social insurance programmes means that the federal government's redirection of resources across generations will grow much larger over time. This pattern is no different in many European countries, including the UK.

---

1 Federal outlays not reduced by offsetting receipts such as Medicare premiums, federal receipts on employee Social Security, civilian retirement and military retirement, and so on.

2 Total federal transfer payments were expected to constitute 64 per cent of total expenditures in fiscal year 2012: by 2022, their share will increase to 72 per cent.

It is well known that governments redistribute income and wealth across economic classes – from high earners and the rich towards low-income and poor groups, for example. During coming decades, however, governments' role in redistributing resources from working adults, younger children and unborn generations towards older generations (primarily toward retirees) will also grow larger.

Indeed, it could be argued that the chief reason for the government's dire fiscal outlook is its deep involvement in inter-generational resource redistribution. However, most of the oxygen in the public debate about the role of government in society is exhausted by discussion of the government's role in redistributing resources intra-generationally, from economically well-off citizens towards others. Indeed, the discussion about the latter provides the politically polarising fuel that prevents any rational discussion about the former.

This is similar to the problem represented in the well-known 'prisoner's dilemma' game. If political parties – just two parties in the US – could agree to a deal on entitlement reform – to effectively save and invest resources for the future needs of an ageing population rather than just making promises to pay benefits out of future tax revenues – and are able to faithfully sustain and execute that promise, the economic benefits to the public in terms of an equitable inter-generational allocation of resources and efficient economic incentives would be immense. However, individual political parties tend to be distrustful of each other and this is certainly the case in the US. Both Democrats and Republicans believe that agreeing to such a deal would risk the loss of political power (too many of their supporters may become disappointed) and the deal would then be undercut when the opposing party gains power – by the squandering of any accrued savings on the current redistributive priorities of the governing party. The Democrats might agree to long-term reform if they knew that the Republicans would not spend the savings on expanding their favourite programmes when they came into office and vice versa.

Unfortunately, delaying a deal increases the size of the 'fiscal cliff' and increases the hurdles policymakers must surmount to make a deal. The longer there is delay, the more the costs accumulate. The fact that official budget agencies are refusing to report the implicit debts embedded in long-term entitlement programmes that will eventually involve huge resource transfers from future to current generations allows the lop-sided emphasis on intra-generational issues to dominate.

This study, which updates calculations of federal fiscal and generational imbalances and reports generational accounts under current fiscal policies, shows that the window of opportunity for a workable fiscal grand bargain between the two major US political parties is shrinking rapidly. The same is true in European countries.

US Congressional Budget Office's projections: 'baseline' versus 'alternative'

The US federal government's fiscal situation is dire. According to the non-partisan CBO, this fiscal year's gap between tax receipts and federal spending will be \$1.2 trillion, or almost 8 per cent of the nation's GDP.[3] The cumulative deficit under the CBO's 'baseline' projections – under which currently scheduled laws governing taxes and expenditures are assumed to be fully implemented – is projected at $2.9 trillion over ten years (2013–22). However, the CBO's ten-year baseline projection is not credible. The US Congress has consistently enacted exceptions to scheduled tax and spending laws in order to prevent economic harm to particular political interest groups (for example, doctors or middle-class taxpayers) and it will almost certainly do so again. Therefore, the CBO also includes 'alternative' scenarios in its budget reports. One of these suggests a ten-year cumulative deficit of $10.7 trillion.[4]

The expenditure cuts and tax increases scheduled under the baseline policy path would reduce future deficits by $7.8 trillion ($10.7 trillion minus $2.9 trillion) over the next ten years compared with the alternative policy path where those changes are postponed until after 2022. Thus, if Congress continues its past practice of postponing the adoption of current fiscal policies, those of us alive during the next ten years will enjoy a $7.8 trillion boost to our resources. We will pay a net $7.8 trillion less for the public benefits of external defence, security, infrastructure construction, research and development, and so on. The additional $7.8 trillion of the payment for those public goods

---

3   See 'Updated Budget Projections: Fiscal Years 2012–2022', Congressional Budget Office, March 2012. Available at http://www.cbo.gov/publication/43119.

4   The CBO reports mention that the baseline is only a benchmark against which to compare alternative policy choices.

and services – that we will enjoy – will have to be picked up by future generations of taxpayers. This will happen either through smaller federal direct benefits (transfer payments) or higher federal taxes.

The longer Congress continues to allow the gap between federal taxes and benefits to persist, the larger the gap will grow as it accrues interest, at about 3.7 per cent per year today as indicated by the real interest rate on the government's long-term securities. It means that we will consume $7.8 trillion of the nation's income through extra government 'benefits' that we will not 'pay' for.[5] The accumulated additional federal debt will then constitute a bill that will be presented to those alive after 2022. Some of these people will, of course, have been alive in 2010 but some will have died; and there will be new entrants into the workforce – young workers and immigrants – who will bear these costs.

The generational implications of the CBO's ten-year budget projections: 2013–22

As noted above, Congress has frequently intervened during the last decade to prevent, postpone or alter the

---

5 The terms 'benefits' and 'pay' are in quotes because of their ambiguity. 'Benefits' include those provided through loopholes in income tax laws or through 'temporary' reductions in tax rates. And 'payments' to the federal government could take the form of direct tax increases, loophole eliminations, direct benefit cuts or increases in taxes on benefits, stricter (less generous) eligibility conditions for benefit programs, and so on.

implementation of particular tax and expenditure laws to protect the interests of specific groups – the Medicare 'docfix' for preventing steep cuts to physician reimbursements and the indexation of Alternative Minimum Tax (AMT) rate brackets to protect middle-class taxpayers, and so on. However, at the time of writing, the stakes are considerably higher than simply preserving the interests of particular citizen groups, although those concerns remain relevant. Beyond concerns with the AMT and Medicare physician's reimbursements, all Americans are facing economic jeopardy from the fiscal cliff that has been created under current tax laws. This crisis keeps reappearing in different guises such as the expiry, at the end of 2012, of the George W. Bush era tax cuts; the sizeable automatic spending cuts scheduled for early 2013 under the Deficit Control Act of 2011; and the more recent 'stand-off' between the president and Congress.[6] If allowed, politicians will fear that raising taxes and reducing federal expenditures could create a large fiscal drag on the economy, boosting unemployment and tipping the economy into another recession.

It is because of the near certainty that Congress will seek to avoid the economic consequences of allowing current tax and spending laws to be fully implemented that the CBO reports two sets of federal budget projections. As

---

6   The automatic spending cuts were delayed for three months (Under Public Law 112-240) before they went into force after March 31, 2013. But Congress again reversed course under the Bipartisan Budget Act of December 2013, providing two-year $63 billion relief from the automatic spending cuts.

Table 1   **Potential changes to scheduled 'current law' fiscal policies**

Policy	Cumulative increase in deficit (2013–22) $ billions
Maintain Medicare physician payments at current rates	316
Extend expiring tax provisions*	3,557
Index AMT income limits to inflation*	1,008
Remove BCA2011 automatic sequester: Defence discretionary§	539
Remove BCA2011 automatic sequester: Non-defence mandatory: Medicare	132
Remove BCA2011 automatic sequester: Non-defence mandatory: Other†	52
Remove BCA2011 automatic sequester: Non-defence discretionary§	356
Total direct effect on federal debt	5,960

* Assumes extension of expiring tax provisions and adjustments to AMT limits will be implemented together. This excludes consideration of the partial employee payroll tax rate reduction for 2011–12.
† Excludes Social Security, Medicaid and other programmes exempt from DCA sequester.
§ Elimination of sequester automatic spending cut not assumed to affect taxes and transfers of current generations.

Source: Fiscal year totals based on CBO's January 2012 Budget Outlook. 'BCA2011' stands for Budget Control Act of 2011.

noted, the 'baseline projection' assumes implementation of current laws and the 'alternative projection' assumes elimination of certain parts of current tax and spending laws that would prevent federal tax increases and spending cuts.

Table 2   **Ten-year generational accounts by selected age and gender: 2013–22 (present values of net taxes in $000s 2012 dollars)**

| | Baseline projection | | Alternative projection* | | Difference | |
Age	Males (1)	Females (2)	Males (3)	Females (4)	Males (5) = (1) – (3)	Females (6) = (2) – (4)
0	−15.6	−15.4	−15.6	−15.4	0.0	0.0
10	−11.3	−11.8	−11.5	−11.9	0.2	0.1
20	61.4	38.1	56.0	36.4	5.4	1.7
30	135.8	77.1	117.5	63.3	18.3	13.8
40	163.2	104.2	131.4	84.0	31.8	20.2
50	159.5	111.4	126.5	93.7	33.0	17.7
60	−1.3	−13.5	−35.3	−23.6	34.0	10.1
70	−168.3	−150.9	−184.3	−157.4	16.0	6.5
80	−166.2	−146.2	−172.2	−150.6	6.0	4.4
90	−107.2	−98.4	−109.7	−101.1	2.5	2.7

* Includes the effects of all items in Table 1 except automatic sequester defence and non-defence discretionary spending changes. The two latter items are cumulatively projected to be $895 billion during 2013–22.

Source: Author's calculations.

Table 1 lists the policies under the baseline that would be changed if the alternative policy scenario were to be followed instead. It also shows the direct cumulative change in the debt between 2013 and 2022 (in undiscounted nominal dollars excluding debt service reductions) associated with each of the policies. Table 1 shows that the direct effect of postponing or removing from current laws the policy items mentioned would be to cumulatively add almost $6 trillion to the federal debt by 2022.[7]

Given the ten-year budget horizon adopted by the US Congress, it is useful to know how shifting from baseline to alternative policies would affect individuals' budgets over just the next ten years.[8] Columns 2–5 of Table 2 show the actuarial present value of net taxes (taxes minus transfers received), estimated for people of selected ages by gender, under baseline and alternative fiscal policies from 2013 to 2022. Population projections provided by the Social Security Administration and several micro-data profiles of tax and transfer payments are used to show the distribution of CBO aggregate projections up to 2022 on a per-capita basis. These are labelled Ten-Year Forward Generational Accounts.[9] The estimates are actuarial present values calculated using an inflation-adjusted discount rate of 3.7 per cent per year and age-specific cohort mortality rates.[10]

---

7   According to CBO's projections, additional ten-year debt service costs under the alternative projection would be $1.9 trillion compared with those under the baseline projection.

8   Of course, continuing baseline or alternative policies beyond ten years will also affect individuals' budgets. Those effects are described in Table 3 later in the main text.

9   Figures that show age–gender distributions of various federal taxes and transfers are available from the author upon request.

10 The discount rate applied to calculate present values equals the interest rate on the government's longest-maturity (30-year) treasury securities. That current rate turns out to be very close to the discount rate used in earlier fiscal and generational accounting

Columns 1 and 2 of Table 2 show the age–gender distribution of the present value of net tax payments under the CBO's baseline projections. The table shows that very young individuals and those aged 60 and older will be recipients of net government transfers during the next ten years, whereas working-age adults younger than 60 will pay more taxes than they will receive in transfers from the government through to the year 2022. Columns 3 and 4 of Table 2 show the same information as the first two columns of the table, but under the CBO's alternative budget projection.

Under both baseline and alternative projections, the most significant concurrent public inter-generational transfers during the next ten years will occur between adult middle-aged workers and retirees. For example, under the alternative policies (column 3), 40-year-old males are projected to surrender to the federal government about $131,400 in present value terms, on average, during the next decade; and 70-year-old male retirees will receive $184,300 in present value terms, on average, between 2013 and 2022. As is well known, this redistribution – a ten-year segment of projected federal transactions – occurs primarily through Social Security and Medicare taxes paid by workers to fund those programmes' benefit payments to

estimates of 3.67 per cent. The mortality adjustment applied when calculating actuarial present values of a future tax payment – say, at age 50 in 2023 by a male aged 40 in 2013 – is implemented by applying the ratio of the projected population of 50-year-old males in 2023 to the population of 40-year-old males in 2013.

retirees.[11] It is worth pointing out that prospective generational accounts ignore past tax payments made by today's retirees. However, the main use of generational accounts is to reveal the future implications of policy changes as discussed below.

Because the alternative projection eliminates from the baseline those policies that would increase taxes or reduce transfers and government purchases, it results in reduced taxes and increased transfers for almost all generations. Columns 5 and 6 of Table 2 show the actuarial-present-value difference for different generations between baseline and alternative projections. The present value of the increased resources over the ten-year period for today's 40-year-old males is $31,800 per capita on average; the figure is $20,200 for 40-year-old females. The increases in the present value of net resources vary for different age and gender groups because they reflect different direct tax-transfer incidences of the policies that are changed between the baseline and the alternative scenarios. For both males and females, younger adult generations and retirees would receive smaller boosts to their resources during the next ten years under the CBO's alternative policy path.

In addition, today's generations will reap the benefits of higher government purchases of pure public goods and services – defence and non-defence discretionary

---

11 Detailed results show that excluding Social Security and Medicare taxes and transfers from the Ten-Year Generational Account calculations would eliminate almost all of the inter-generational transfers from working adults toward retirees.

programmes – totalling $895 billion over ten years.[12] Normally, policies to provide extra public goods should be funded by the generations that will benefit from them. However, shifting from baseline to alternative policies involves providing current generations with more public goods and services, but also more transfers and lower taxes. The taxes that will be required to pay for those additional public goods will be imposed on future generations.

Tables 1 and 2 capture the dilemma that US policymakers face. Given their past actions to reduce, postpone or prevent policies that are enshrined in current law from being implemented, it is likely to happen again. Following the alternative policy path – or a slight variation thereof – may avoid the short-term consequences of adjustment but will also award sizeable additional resources and public benefits to today's generations at the expense of a $7.8 trillion increase in the nation's debt burden (around $6 trillion in direct policy effects and $1.9 in additional debt service). This is a debt burden that future working and taxpaying generations would have to bear.

On the other hand, despite reducing, preventing and postponing the effects of baseline policies in the past – and, in addition, introducing a partial payroll tax holiday

---

12 These policy changes are not included in the results reported in Table 2 because the benefits of such government purchases accrue to many current and future generations and cannot be allocated exclusively across today's age–gender cohorts. The net taxes shown in Table 2 indicate how each current generation's direct payments net of receipts contributes towards funding such pure public goods and services.

since late 2010 – GDP growth has remained sluggish and employment growth has remained slow. If this experience continues during the next year or two, the adoption of the alternative fiscal policy path may accrue additional debt without delivering the expected short-term beneficial effects of economic growth.[13] Indeed, continuing on the alternative policy path and continuing to accumulate debt at a rapid pace may eventually bring about those very effects on output and employment that policymakers are currently seeking to avoid.

Although the resource redistribution trade-offs under alternative policy choices are understood in general terms, their implications, on average, for individual workers, consumers and retirees are not explicitly calculated and reported by official budget-reporting agencies. Without such supplementary budget metrics, fiscal policy debates remain bereft of important information that could help lawmakers better calibrate national fiscal policy choices.

The long-term generational implications of baseline and alternative US fiscal paths

Of course, the world is unlikely to end in the year 2022 – the last year of the CBO's current ten-year budget window.

---

13 The effectiveness of the fiscal stimulus provided under alternative policies relative to baseline policies depends at least partly on whether today's generations are 'Ricardian' in their consumption–saving response. In other words, will current generations reduce their consumption in anticipation of future higher taxes to service the additional debt that is incurred? This is an issue beyond the scope of this monograph.

What would be the implications of extending the baseline scenarios under current laws and also the alternative scenario policies beyond 2022? Although the CBO is not legally required to do so, it occasionally publishes reports on long-range budget projections to show prospective aggregate federal receipts and expenditures and their implications over several additional decades. Again, however, the generational implications of those paths remain unreported and unappreciated. Not having access to a sufficiently detailed set of long-range receipts and expenditures on federal tax and transfer programmes, this study extends and re-orientates the CBO's ten-year baseline and alternative policy paths to estimate their inter-generational impact. Population projections provided by the Social Security Administration and several micro-data based profiles of tax and transfer payments are used to project the per-capita estimates for the year 2022. The values of taxes and transfers by age and gender are adjusted upward for each future year at the CBO's long-term annual productivity growth rate assumptions.[14] However, various health care benefits are adjusted at a faster rate of growth than economy-wide productivity plus population growth – consistent with historical evidence.[15]

---

14 The growth rate of real wages is given in The 2012 Long Term Budget Outlook, Congressional Budget Office, supplemental data EXCEL file, June 2012. Available at http://www.cbo.gov/sites/all/themes/cbo/images/document-icons/XLS_ic.png.

15 The faster rate of growth for Medicare Part A is taken from growth rate differentials relative to payroll base growth reported by the Medicare Trustees through to 2035. See Table IV.A2 in the

Generational accounts are calculated as actuarial present values of taxes paid minus transfers received per capita during a person's remaining lifetime. As in the previous section, projected taxes and transfers are discounted at an inflation-adjusted discount rate of about 3.7 per cent per year adjusted for mortality.

Table 3 shows generational accounts at selected ages for the 2013 US population by gender under federal baseline and alternative policies. The generational account of a 40-year-old male under alternative policies is just $37,600 per year. Table 2 (column 3) shows that the ten-year present value of net taxes for a 40-year-old male in 2013 is much larger: $131,400. The difference arises because the present value of future Social Security, Medicare and other benefits after 2022, in years beyond the person's 50th birthday, exceed his tax payments after 2022 by an amount equal to the difference between the two estimates: $93,800.

2012 Medicare Trustees' annual report. Available at http://www
.cms.gov/Research-Statistics-Data-and-Systems/Statistics
-Trends-and-Reports/ReportsTrustFunds/Downloads/TR2012.
pdf. An 'intensity allowance' adjustment factor, required by the
Affordable Care Act of 2010 and also reported by the Medicare
Trustees, is included in the growth adjustment differential. Beyond
2035, the Medicare Part A cost differential is gradually decreased
until per-capita expenditure growth equals economy-wide productivity growth. For Medicare Part B, the trustees report growth
rate differentials relative to GDP growth: see Table II.F2 in the 2012
Medicare Trustees' annual report. Target growth rates are selected
for the time segments through to 2085 to deliver identical growth
rate differentials relative to GDP growth to calibrate growth of future SMI expenditures.

Table 3 **Lifetime generational accounts as of fiscal year 2013 by selected age and gender (present values of net taxes in $000s 2012 dollars)**

Age	Baseline projection Males (1)	Baseline projection Females (2)	Alternative projection* Males (3)	Alternative projection* Females (4)	Difference Males (5) = (1) − (3)	Difference Females (6) = (2) − (4)
0	150.4	23.4	76.8	−19.3	73.6	42.7
10	211.3	58.9	122.2	7.1	89.1	51.8
20	271.1	95.7	168.9	38.3	102.2	57.4
30	246.3	74.0	138.2	14.8	108.1	59.2
40	140.2	10.3	37.6	−38.6	102.6	48.9
50	−15.6	−92.8	−98.6	−125.7	83.0	32.9
60	−213.1	−232.3	−269.4	−250.8	56.3	18.5
70	−285.4	−273.2	−309.3	−283.9	23.9	10.7
80	−198.1	−184.1	−205.8	−189.8	7.7	5.7
90	−109.4	−102.4	−111.9	−105.2	2.5	2.8

* Includes the effects of continuing alternative policies – all items in Table 1 except automatic sequester defence and non-defence discretionary spending.

Source: Author's calculations.

Women's generational accounts are generally smaller than those of males of corresponding ages because they work and earn less than men and they live and collect benefits for longer. For 40-year-old women, the difference between their alternative generational account (Table 3, $84,000) and alternative ten-year account (Table 2, −$38,600) equals $122,000. It is also larger than the difference for 40-year-old men, again because women will pay fewer taxes and are likely to receive benefits for longer after 2022 compared with men because of their greater longevity.

Table 3 shows that if alternative policies are continued beyond the next ten years, they would impose considerably smaller fiscal burdens on today's generations compared with baseline policies. For example, the lifetime resource increase for today's 30-year-old males and females – who are about to enter their peak working and earning years – would be $108,100 and $59,200, respectively. All generations, including younger retirees, would receive a significant boost to their lifetime resources as a result of adopting the alternative fiscal path in the long term compared with the baseline policy path. Under alternative policies, today's generations would also receive additional benefits from larger federal public goods provision through discretionary federal spending – benefits that are not reflected in the estimates in Table 3. This indicates the difficulty of moving towards more conservative fiscal policies: most of today's voters gain considerably from lower taxes and higher benefits.

6   THE US FEDERAL FISCAL IMBALANCE

As discussed earlier, the fiscal imbalance measure of the federal government's financial condition when calculated in perpetuity fully characterises the underlying set of tax and expenditure policies: it helps us understand much better the long-term financial implications of current policy. The fiscal imbalance calculation discounts future fiscal deficits (non-interest expenditures minus receipts) at the government's long-term interest rate.[1] The resulting estimate – expressed in constant 2012 dollars in this study – shows the amount of additional funds that the government would need, invested at interest, to pay for all future fiscal deficits under the given set of policies. Alternatively, it is the additional amount of resources the government needs now if it is never to change policy.[2]

The last row of Table 4 shows that under baseline policies the federal government's 2012 fiscal imbalance, measured in constant 2012 dollars, equals $54.4 trillion. This

---

1   The discounted sum of future deficits converges to a finite number because in a normal economic environment (technically known as dynamic efficiency) the discount rate is larger than the economy's growth rate (see Abel et al. 1989).

2   The full derivation and explanation of the fiscal imbalance measure is available in Gokhale and Smetters (2003).

Table 4   The federal government's fiscal imbalance under baseline policies (beginning-of-fiscal-year present values in billions of constant 2012 dollars)

	2012	2013	2014	2015	2016	2017	2018	2019	2020	2021	2022
Social insurance fiscal imbalance	**64,853**	**65,352**	**66,710**	**68,112**	**69,534**	**70,961**	**73,180**	**75,458**	**77,775**	**80,146**	**82,564**
Future imbalance	67,826	68,308	69,640	71,020	72,428	73,846	76,061	78,345	80,655	83,007	85,397
Trust funds	2,973	2,956	2,930	2,908	2,894	2,885	2,881	2,887	2,880	2,861	2,833
Rest of government fiscal imbalance	**−10,502**	**−10,233**	**−10,339**	**−10,502**	**−10,641**	**−10,687**	**−10,994**	**−11,257**	**−11,460**	**−11,619**	**−11,742**
Future imbalance	−23,603	−24,368	−24,937	−25,324	−25,555	−25,692	−25,987	−26,211	−26,394	−26,521	−26,597
Liabilities to the public	10,128	11,179	11,668	11,914	12,020	12,120	12,112	12,067	12,054	12,041	12,022
Liabilities to trust funds	2,973	2,956	2,930	2,908	2,894	2,885	2,881	2,887	2,880	2,861	2,833
Federal fiscal imbalance	**54,351**	**55,119**	**56,371**	**57,610**	**58,893**	**60,274**	**62,186**	**64,201**	**66,315**	**68,527**	**70,822**

Source: Author's calculations.

Table 5 **The federal government's fiscal imbalance under alternative policies**
(beginning-of-fiscal-year present values in billions of constant 2012 dollars)

	2012	2013	2014	2015	2016	2017	2018	2019	2020	2021	2022
Social insurance fiscal imbalance	**65,934**	**66,440**	**67,804**	**69,201**	**70,619**	**72,036**	**74,256**	**76,529**	**78,841**	**81,202**	**83,606**
Future imbalance	68,907	69,396	70,734	72,109	73,513	74,921	77,137	79,416	81,721	84,063	86,439
Trust funds	2,973	2,956	2,930	2,908	2,894	2,885	2,881	2,887	2,880	2,861	2,833
Rest of government fiscal imbalance	**25,457**	**26,261**	**27,076**	**27,919**	**28,810**	**29,826**	**30,994**	**32,256**	**33,631**	**35,101**	**36,660**
Future imbalance	12,356	12,103	12,081	12,168	12,401	12,736	13,306	13,966	14,685	15,472	16,323
Liabilities to the public	10,128	11,202	12,065	12,843	13,515	14,205	14,807	15,403	16,066	16,768	17,504
Liabilities to trust funds	2,973	2,956	2,930	2,908	2,894	2,885	2,881	2,887	2,880	2,861	2,833
Federal fiscal imbalance	**91,391**	**92,701**	**94,880**	**97,120**	**99,429**	**101,862**	**105,250**	**108,785**	**112,472**	**116,303**	**120,266**

Source: Author's calculations.

figure comprises a fiscal imbalance of $64.8 trillion from the two major social insurance programmes – Social Security and Medicare – and a negative fiscal imbalance on account of the rest of federal programmes of –$10.5 trillion. The total fiscal imbalance is around four times the official national debt held by the public.

Under the alternative policy path – shown in the last row of Table 5 – the 2012 federal fiscal imbalance is $91.4 trillion, with almost all of the increase coming from the rest-of-government operations which now contribute $25.5 trillion to the estimate. The $37.0 trillion swing results from adopting the alternative policy path rather than the baseline path and maintaining that choice indefinitely into the future.

Even under baseline policies, the federal government's financial condition appears dire. Ironically, the immediate challenge perceived by policymakers is about how to avoid the so-called 'fiscal cliff' – that is, how to hew closely to the alternative policy path and avoid the immediate negative economic effects that will follow if the CBO's baseline policy path is followed. The reality is that if the US does follow the CBO's alternative path and does not take action to put government finances on a more secure long-term footing, the position will become more unstable over time. The focus of our discussion will be on the fiscal imbalance as measured in 2012. However, Tables 4–9, which are discussed further in the following section, also show how the numbers will evolve from 2012 if no policy action is taken.

Various methods of presenting the fiscal imbalance

Since the dollar values of the fiscal imbalance estimates are extremely large it is helpful to present them in different ways. It is common to see total public debt, including future social security obligations, presented as a proportion of one-year's national income. This is convenient because it is how explicit government debt is presented in comparisons across different countries, and it requires fewer assumptions to produce the measures. It is also the case that, in the personal debt market, we often see mortgage debt for individuals presented in the same way. However, such a presentation is misleading. The fiscal imbalance is a measure of the long-term gap between revenues and expenditures given current policies. It will not be – and could not be – made good out of one year's national income. Also, different countries may grow at different rates (for example, because of immigration, different regulatory environments and so on) and therefore could reasonably cope with different levels of debt as a percentage of current national income. For similar reasons, it is also not helpful to measure fiscal imbalances as a sum per head. Instead, fiscal imbalance measures are better expressed as ratios of the present value of future gross domestic product (GDP) (see Tables 6 and 7) or of future payrolls (see Tables 8 and 9).[3] Payrolls may approximate

---

3   Clearly, GDP and payroll projections should also be different under baseline and alternative policy paths. However, the CBO does not

Table 6 **The federal government's fiscal imbalance under baseline policies as a percentage of the present value of GDP (beginning-of-fiscal-year values)**

	2012	2013	2014	2015	2016	2017	2018	2019	2020	2021	2022
Social insurance fiscal imbalance	**6.4**	**6.3**	**6.3**	**6.4**	**6.4**	**6.4**	**6.4**	**6.5**	**6.6**	**6.7**	**6.7**
Future imbalance	6.7	6.6	6.6	6.6	6.6	6.6	6.7	6.8	6.8	6.9	7.0
Trust funds	0.3	0.3	0.3	0.3	0.3	0.3	0.3	0.2	0.3	0.2	0.2
Rest of government fiscal imbalance	**−1.0**	**−1.0**	**−1.0**	**−1.0**	**−1.0**	**−1.0**	**−1.0**	**−1.0**	**−1.0**	**−1.0**	**−1.0**
Future imbalance	−2.3	−2.4	−2.4	−2.4	−2.3	−2.3	−2.3	−2.3	−2.2	−2.2	−2.2
Liabilities to the public	1.0	1.1	1.1	1.1	1.1	1.1	1.1	1.0	1.0	1.0	1.0
Liabilities to trust funds	0.3	0.3	0.3	0.3	0.3	0.3	0.3	0.2	0.3	0.2	0.2
Federal fiscal imbalance	**5.4**	**5.4**	**5.4**	**5.4**	**5.4**	**5.4**	**5.5**	**5.5**	**5.6**	**5.7**	**5.8**

Source: Author's calculations.

Table 7 **The federal government's fiscal imbalance under alternative policies as a percentage of the present value of GDP (beginning-of-fiscal-year values)**

	2012	2013	2014	2015	2016	2017	2018	2019	2020	2021	2022
Social insurance fiscal imbalance	**6.5**	**6.5**	**6.4**	**6.5**	**6.5**	**6.5**	**6.5**	**6.6**	**6.7**	**6.7**	**6.8**
Future imbalance	6.8	6.7	6.7	6.7	6.7	6.7	6.8	6.8	6.9	7.0	7.1
Trust funds	0.3	0.3	0.3	0.3	0.3	0.3	0.3	0.2	0.3	0.2	0.2
Rest of government fiscal imbalance	**2.5**	**2.6**	**2.6**	**2.6**	**2.6**	**2.7**	**2.7**	**2.8**	**2.9**	**2.9**	**3.0**
Future imbalance	1.2	1.2	1.2	1.1	1.1	1.2	1.2	1.2	1.2	1.3	1.3
Liabilities to the public	1.0	1.1	1.2	1.2	1.2	1.3	1.3	1.3	1.4	1.4	1.4
Liabilities to trust funds	0.3	0.3	0.3	0.3	0.3	0.3	0.3	0.2	0.3	0.2	0.2
Federal fiscal imbalance	**9.0**	**9.0**	**9.0**	**9.1**	**9.1**	**9.1**	**9.2**	**9.4**	**9.5**	**9.7**	**9.8**

Source: Author's calculations.

more closely to the tax base that could be used to make good the fiscal imbalance.

Table 6 shows that eliminating the fiscal imbalance calculated by assuming that baseline policies will be followed would take up 5.4 per cent of all future GDP. But the required sacrifice would be much larger – 9.0 per cent of all future GDP – under the alternative path, which better represents the current policy direction and a more realistic assessment of the future policy direction.[4] These ratio fiscal imbalance metrics show the size of policy changes that are required – that policymakers must today enact and maintain throughout the future – to shift the trajectory of future federal expenditures and receipts from those projected under the two different policy paths to eliminate the fiscal imbalance. The policy shift must ultimately be sufficient to reduce the imbalance between projected federal receipts and expenditures to zero. That is, the government must ultimately fully pay for what it spends. The government must raise taxes or cut spending by 5.4 per cent of

---

provide alternative paths for GDP and payrolls under alternative policy assumptions. Here, too, GDP and total payrolls are projected only under the baseline policy assumption. Strictly speaking, the ratio measures of the fiscal imbalance should be interpreted as the amount of future output (or payrolls) under baseline policies that would have to be sacrificed to eliminate the fiscal imbalance under the alternative policy path.

4   If we did quote the imbalance as a per cent of current annual GDP, under baseline policies, the fiscal imbalance of $54.4 trillion amounts to 350 per cent of fiscal year 2012 GDP. Under alternative policies, the $91.4 trillion fiscal imbalance translates to 589 per cent of fiscal year 2012 GDP.

GDP as compared with the assumptions in the current US budget. If the alternative policy plan is followed, then the government must cut spending or raise taxes by 9 per cent of GDP if all expenditures are to be met through taxation: it must do so now and maintain that increase forever. The government could, of course, delay the adjustment. However, the longer it is delayed, the bigger the ultimate adjustment will have to be.

To some observers, a fiscal imbalance of about 9 per cent of GDP under the alternative path may appear to be manageable. However, the nation's entire GDP is not subject to taxes. If it is assumed that the fiscal imbalance will be made good by tax increases and if total payrolls are taken as the appropriate base, the additional taxes required on payrolls to eliminate the fiscal imbalance beginning in 2012 would be 11.7 per cent of payrolls under baseline policies (see Table 8) and 19.7 per cent of payrolls under the alternative path (see Table 9). This is an indication of the rise in taxes that would be needed to meet current spending obligations if it took place now and was implemented forever. The compelling statistic, perhaps, is that resolving the fiscal imbalance implies more than a doubling of federal payroll taxes from current levels under the alternative policy path. If Congress decides to follow the CBO's alternative policy path, as it has tended to in the past, rather than the baseline path, a tax increase of an additional 8.0 percentage points of payrolls is necessary in the long term to fund the additional spending. It is worth noting that the difference between the baseline and alternative scenarios arises from differences in rest-of-government spending

Table 8 **The federal government's fiscal imbalance under baseline policies as a percentage of the present value of uncapped payrolls (beginning-of-fiscal-year values)**

	2012	2013	2014	2015	2016	2017	2018	2019	2020	2021	2022
Social insurance fiscal imbalance	**14.0**	**13.8**	**13.8**	**13.8**	**13.8**	**13.8**	**14.0**	**14.1**	**14.3**	**14.5**	**14.6**
Future imbalance	14.6	14.4	14.4	14.4	14.4	14.4	14.5	14.7	14.8	15.0	15.1
Trust funds	0.6	0.6	0.6	0.6	0.6	0.6	0.6	0.6	0.5	0.5	0.5
Rest of government fiscal imbalance	**−2.3**	**−2.2**	**−2.1**	**−2.1**	**−2.1**	**−2.1**	**−2.1**	**−2.1**	**−2.1**	**−2.1**	**−2.1**
Future imbalance	−5.1	−5.2	−5.2	−5.1	−5.1	−5.0	−5.0	−4.9	−4.9	−4.8	−4.7
Liabilities to the public	2.2	2.4	2.4	2.4	2.4	2.4	2.3	2.3	2.2	2.2	2.1
Liabilities to trust funds	0.6	0.6	0.6	0.6	0.6	0.6	0.6	0.6	0.5	0.5	0.5
Federal fiscal imbalance	**11.7**	**11.6**	**11.7**	**11.7**	**11.7**	**11.7**	**11.9**	**12.0**	**12.2**	**12.4**	**12.5**

Source: Author's calculations.

Table 9 The federal government's fiscal imbalance under alternative policies as a percentage of the present value of uncapped payrolls (beginning-of-fiscal-year values)

	2012	2013	2014	2015	2016	2017	2018	2019	2020	2021	2022
Social insurance fiscal imbalance	**14.2**	**14.1**	**14.0**	**14.0**	**14.0**	**14.0**	**14.2**	**14.3**	**14.5**	**14.6**	**14.8**
Future imbalance	14.9	14.7	14.6	14.6	14.6	14.6	14.7	14.9	15.0	15.2	15.3
Trust funds	0.6	0.6	0.6	0.6	0.6	0.6	0.6	0.6	0.5	0.5	0.5
Rest of government fiscal imbalance	**5.5**	**5.6**	**5.6**	**5.7**	**5.7**	**5.8**	**5.9**	**6.1**	**6.2**	**6.3**	**6.5**
Future imbalance	2.7	2.6	2.5	2.5	2.5	2.5	2.5	2.6	2.7	2.8	2.9
Liabilities to the public	2.2	2.4	2.5	2.6	2.7	2.8	2.8	2.9	3.0	3.0	3.1
Liabilities to trust funds	0.6	0.6	0.6	0.6	0.6	0.6	0.6	0.6	0.5	0.5	0.5
Federal fiscal imbalance	**19.7**	**19.6**	**19.6**	**19.7**	**19.7**	**19.9**	**20.1**	**20.4**	**20.7**	**21.0**	**21.3**

Source: Author's calculations.

rather than differences between the Social Security and Medicare items.

How the fiscal imbalance will evolve

According to Tables 4–9, the current-policy fiscal imbalance will grow larger over time, not only in dollar terms, but also as a ratio of the present value of future GDP or future payrolls. The increases in the fiscal imbalance are explained by the fact that the fiscal imbalance grows larger at the rate of interest whereas GDP and payrolls grow at the generally slower rate of economy-wide productivity growth. Table 9 shows that not shifting from current policies (the CBO's alternative path) for another ten years would increase the size of the required policy adjustment: instead of a permanent payroll tax increase in 2012 of 19.7 per cent being necessary, waiting until 2022 would make the required payroll tax increase 21.3 per cent.

There are a number of ways, in principle, of resolving the fiscal imbalance through future policy changes. A sense of how large the changes would have to be to put US fiscal policy on a long-term sustainable footing is provided in Table 10. When interpreting the numbers in the table, it is especially important to consider the context in the US. The fiscal imbalance that has been calculated relates only to the federal government and there are other layers of government in the US. Therefore, a fiscal imbalance that is equal to what might appear to be a relatively small proportion of future national income might involve a much bigger proportionate increase in federal taxes. On top of this, there will be other layers of government levying their own taxes and which have their own long-term fiscal problems.

Table 10 shows the level of fiscal adjustment that will be required as a ratio of different variables for both the baseline and alternative policy scenarios. The columns show the ratio measure as it will evolve in future years. The first column for year 2012 shows that, even under baseline policies, the fiscal imbalance is already almost as large as the federal government's entire projected discretionary spending (row B10). The table also shows that under the alternative policy path, income taxes would have to be almost doubled or Social Security and Medicare benefits would have to be reduced to about one-tenth of their projected size to eliminate the fiscal imbalance in the long term. Alternatively, it would require increasing all federal receipts by about 50 per cent (row A4) or increasing all income taxes by about 86 per cent (row A5). Eliminating all discretionary expenditures would be insufficient (row A10) to put the US on a long-term sustainable fiscal path.

The contribution of Social Security and Medicare to the US fiscal imbalance

Table 5 showed that the bulk ($65 trillion out of $91 trillion) of the federal fiscal imbalance is attributable to two major social insurance programmes – Social Security and Medicare – that impose taxes on workers to pay for retirement and health care benefits to retired and disabled workers, their dependants and survivors. The obligation

Table 10 **The federal fiscal imbalance as a ratio of various tax and expenditure bases**

(a) CBO baseline federal budget projections

		2012	2013	2014	2015	2016	2017	2018	2019	2020	2021	2022
B1	GDP	5.4	5.3	5.4	5.4	5.4	5.4	5.5	5.5	5.6	5.7	5.8
B2	Payrolls	11.7	11.7	11.7	11.7	11.7	11.7	11.9	12.0	12.2	12.4	12.6
B3	Total expenditures	21.3	21.5	21.7	21.9	22.1	22.3	22.5	22.7	23.0	23.2	23.4
B4	Total federal receipts	25.5	25.8	26.0	26.3	26.6	27.0	27.3	27.6	28.0	28.4	28.8
B5	Income taxes	40.2	40.6	41.0	41.4	41.8	42.4	42.9	43.4	44.0	44.6	45.2
B6	Non-social insurance expenditures	42.9	43.6	44.1	44.5	45.0	45.6	46.1	46.6	47.1	47.6	48.1
B7	Non-social insurance revenues	35.8	36.1	36.5	36.8	37.2	37.7	38.2	38.7	39.2	39.7	40.3
B8	Social Security & Medicare expenditures	51.2	51.7	52.1	52.4	52.8	53.2	53.5	53.9	54.4	54.8	55.3
B9	Social Security & Medicare revenues	88.9	90.0	91.1	92.1	93.3	94.6	95.8	97.1	98.4	99.9	101.3
B10	Discretionary expenditures	87.8	89.6	91.1	92.5	93.9	95.4	96.7	98.1	99.5	100.9	102.3
B11	Mandatory expenditures	28.0	28.3	28.5	28.7	28.9	29.2	29.4	29.6	29.8	30.1	30.4

Source: Author's calculations.

(b) CBO alternative federal budget projections

		2012	2013	2014	2015	2016	2017	2018	2019	2020	2021	2022
A1	GDP	9.0	9.0	9.0	9.1	9.1	9.1	9.2	9.4	9.5	9.7	9.8
A2	Payrolls	19.7	19.6	19.6	19.7	19.8	19.8	20.1	20.4	20.7	21.0	21.3
A3	Total expenditures	35.0	35.4	35.8	36.1	36.5	37.0	37.3	37.7	38.1	38.5	38.9
A4	Total federal receipts	50.3	50.9	51.5	52.1	52.9	53.7	54.4	55.2	56.0	56.9	57.8
A5	Income taxes	86.3	87.3	88.3	89.3	90.5	91.8	93.1	94.5	95.8	97.3	98.8
A6	Non-social insurance expenditures	68.7	69.8	70.6	71.5	72.4	73.4	74.3	75.1	76.0	76.9	77.8
A7	Non-social insurance revenues	74.7	75.7	76.5	77.5	78.5	79.7	80.8	81.9	83.1	84.4	85.6
A8	Social Security & Medicare expenditures	86.6	87.4	88.1	88.9	89.6	90.5	91.2	92.0	92.9	93.8	94.7
A9	Social Security & Medicare revenues	153.4	155.4	157.4	159.6	161.9	164.4	166.8	169.3	171.9	174.6	177.4
A10	Discretionary expenditures	136.4	139.1	141.4	143.8	146.2	148.5	150.9	153.1	155.4	157.7	160.0
A11	Mandatory expenditures	47.0	47.5	47.9	48.3	48.7	49.2	49.6	50.0	50.5	51.0	51.5

Source: Author's calculations.

to pay these benefits in the future far outstrips projected revenues under the programmes' current rules. Table 11 separates the social insurance component of the federal government's fiscal imbalance into several sub-components: Social Security, Medicare hospital insurance (HI), Medicare supplementary medical insurance (SMI), Medicare prescription drug (Part D). For each component, Table 11 shows the total imbalance in respect of past and living generations – which equals the future imbalance on account of living generations minus the value of the programme's trust fund – and the imbalance in respect of future generations. For each year, the sum of the fiscal imbalances for these four programmes equals the 'social insurance fiscal imbalance' of Table 5, which is repeated in the first row of Table 11 (the figures differ slightly because of rounding).

Social Security contributes only one-third of the total social insurance fiscal imbalance, with Medicare accounting for the remainder: $45.9 trillion.[5] Table 12 shows the figures as a ratio of the present value of total payrolls: the total social insurance fiscal imbalance was equal to 14.2

---

5   Under an alternative view, Medicare Parts B and D are funded out of general revenues. Some analysts assume this to mean that those Medicare expenditures are intended to be 'first in line' to be funded out of federal general revenues, meaning that Medicare's imbalance calculation should generate a smaller figure. Besides the questionable assumption involved in this argument, it is clear that such a reduction in Medicare's fiscal imbalance would be simply transferred to the rest-of-government's contribution to the fiscal imbalance, leaving the overall imbalance estimate unchanged.

per cent in 2012 and will rise to 14.8 per cent by 2022 if no adjustments are made to the programme. Resolving this imbalance would require approximately doubling the current 15.3 per cent payroll tax.[6] It is interesting to note that the proportion of the fiscal imbalance that is attributable to unfunded health-care costs is much less widely discussed than that arising from unfunded pensions in the debates surrounding the long-term fiscal positions of various countries.

Future generations versus current and past generations

Tables 11 and 12 also decompose the fiscal imbalance to show the imbalance of expenditures compared with revenues relating only to 'past and living generations' (excluding future generations).[7] This measure assesses the extent to which today's social insurance policies would provide excess benefits to or, if negative, impose fiscal burdens on, today's generations taken as a whole. This is known as the generational imbalance. By implication, the difference between the fiscal imbalance and the generational imbalance provides an estimate of the net fiscal benefit (or burden) that maintaining a given fiscal policy (either the baseline or alternative policies in this case) would

---

6   Most of the existing Social Security payroll tax is levied on a capped payrolls base which includes about 85 per cent of total payrolls.

7   The generational imbalance measure is also known as the 'closed group' liability measure, that is, the fiscal imbalance measure calculated over the 'closed group' of past and current generations.

Table 11   **The contribution of Social Security and Medicare to the federal fiscal imbalance: CBO alternative projections ($billions)**

(a) Social insurance (Social Security plus Medicare)

	2012	2013	2014	2015	2016	2017	2018	2019	2020	2021	2022
Fiscal imbalance	65,935	66,442	67,805	69,200	70,618	72,036	74,256	76,530	78,841	81,201	83,607
Unfunded obligations: past and living generations	54,074	54,657	55,964	57,306	58,671	60,037	62,083	64,183	66,320	68,501	70,725
Unfunded future obligations: living generations	57,046	57,612	58,894	60,215	61,565	62,922	64,964	67,070	69,199	71,362	73,558
Trust fund	2,973	2,956	2,930	2,908	2,894	2,885	2,881	2,887	2,880	2,861	2,833
Unfunded obligations: future generations	11,861	11,784	11,840	11,894	11,948	11,999	12,173	12,346	12,522	12,701	12,881

(b) Social Security

	2012	2013	2014	2015	2016	2017	2018	2019	2020	2021	2022
Fiscal imbalance	20,077	20,185	20,664	21,185	21,722	22,272	23,101	23,954	24,831	25,733	26,660
Unfunded obligations: past and living generations	19,586	19,686	20,153	20,661	21,187	21,726	22,538	23,375	24,236	25,121	26,032
Unfunded future obligations: living generations	22,240	22,355	22,807	23,288	23,781	24,291	25,065	25,860	26,672	27,496	28,333
Trust fund	2,654	2,669	2,654	2,626	2,594	2,565	2,527	2,485	2,436	2,375	2,301
Unfunded obligations: future generations	491	498	511	523	535	546	563	579	596	612	628

(c) Medicare hospital insurance (Part A)

	2012	2013	2014	2015	2016	2017	2018	2019	2020	2021	2022
Fiscal imbalance	11,483	11,615	11,857	12,096	12,341	12,583	12,961	13,347	13,738	14,143	14,558
Unfunded obligations: past and living generations	11,373	11,552	11,840	12,127	12,419	12,709	13,137	13,574	14,019	14,479	14,949
Unfunded future obligations: living generations	11,618	11,770	12,035	12,299	12,578	12,856	13,279	13,715	14,153	14,601	15,055
Trust fund	246	219	195	172	158	147	142	141	134	122	106
Unfunded obligations: future generations	111	63	17	−30	−78	−126	−176	−228	−281	−335	−391

(d) Medicare supplementary medical insurance (Part B)

	2012	2013	2014	2015	2016	2017	2018	2019	2020	2021	2022
Fiscal imbalance	19,172	19,274	19,581	19,878	20,172	20,462	20,958	21,458	21,963	22,467	22,972
Unfunded obligations: past and living generations	14,411	14,534	14,808	15,072	15,334	15,590	16,003	16,419	16,838	17,254	17,669
Unfunded future obligations: living generations	14,484	14,602	14,889	15,182	15,475	15,763	16,215	16,680	17,147	17,618	18,095
Trust fund	73	68	81	110	142	173	212	261	310	364	426
Unfunded obligations: future generations	4,760	4,740	4,772	4,805	4,839	4,872	4,955	5,039	5,125	5,213	5,302

(e) Medicare prescription drugs (Part D)

	2012	2013	2014	2015	2016	2017	2018	2019	2020	2021	2022
Fiscal imbalance	15,203	15,368	15,703	16,041	16,383	16,719	17,236	17,771	18,309	18,858	19,417
Unfunded obligations: past and living generations	8,704	8,885	9,163	9,446	9,731	10,012	10,405	10,815	1,227	1,647	12,075
Unfunded future obligations: living generations	8,704	8,885	9,163	9,446	9,731	10,012	10,405	10,815	1,227	11,647	12,075
Trust fund	—	—	—	—	—	—	—	—	—	—	—
Unfunded obligations: future generations	6,499	6,483	6,540	6,596	6,652	6,707	6,831	6,956	7,082	7,211	7,342

Source: Author's calculations.

provide (or impose upon) future generations.[8] It is notable that almost the entire Social Security fiscal imbalance reflects an imbalance in favour of past and current generations. Future generations would receive only a small net benefit were current policies continued indefinitely. However, in calculating the imbalance measures as a proportion of payrolls, we are assuming implicitly that the cost of closing the fiscal imbalance is borne by all generations. Furthermore, the longer the adjustment is deferred, the greater will be the proportion of the costs of adjustment that will be imposed on future generations. These figures demonstrate the extent of the inter-generational transfers through pay-as-you-go systems in favour of the current and past generations.

Changes to the fiscal and generational imbalance measures from particular future Social Security policy reforms would indicate how far those policy reforms go in restoring fiscal balance and how fiscally responsible those reforms are. For example, if a reform reduces Social Security's fiscal imbalance by $10 trillion (from $20 to $10 trillion), but the generational imbalance measure is reduced by only $2 trillion, then $8 trillion of the adjustment would be achieved by imposing additional costs on future generations. An alternative reform that achieves the same reduction in the fiscal imbalance but reduces the generational

---

8 Detailed descriptions of generational accounting are provided in Auerbach et al. (1991) and Gokhale (2008). For a description of fiscal and generational imbalance measures, see Gokhale and Smetters (2003).

Table 12   **The contribution of Social Security and Medicare to the federal fiscal imbalance as a percentage of the present value of uncapped payrolls: CBO's alternative projections**

(a) Social insurance (Social Security plus Medicare)

	2012	2013	2014	2015	2016	2017	2018	2019	2020	2021	2022
Fiscal imbalance	14.2	14.0	14.0	14.0	14.0	14.0	14.2	14.3	14.5	14.6	14.8
Unfunded obligations: past and living generations	11.7	11.6	11.6	11.6	11.7	11.7	11.9	12.0	12.2	12.4	12.5
Unfunded future obligations: living generations	12.3	12.2	12.2	12.2	12.2	12.3	12.4	12.6	12.7	12.9	13.0
Trust fund	0.6	0.6	0.6	0.6	0.6	0.6	0.6	0.6	0.5	0.5	0.5
Unfunded obligations: future generations	2.6	2.5	2.5	2.4	2.4	2.4	2.3	2.3	2.3	2.3	2.3
(b) Social Security											
Fiscal imbalance	4.3	4.3	4.3	4.3	4.3	4.3	4.4	4.5	4.6	4.6	4.7
Unfunded obligations: past and living generations	4.2	4.2	4.2	4.2	4.2	4.2	4.3	4.4	4.5	4.5	4.6
Unfunded future obligations: living generations	4.8	4.7	4.7	4.7	4.7	4.7	4.8	4.8	4.9	5.0	5.0
Trust fund	0.6	0.6	0.6	0.5	0.5	0.5	0.5	0.5	0.5	0.4	0.4
Unfunded obligations: future generations	0.1	0.1	0.1	0.1	0.1	0.1	0.1	0.1	0.1	0.1	0.1

(c) Medicare hospital insurance (Part A)

	2012	2013	2014	2015	2016	2017	2018	2019	2020	2021	2022
Fiscal imbalance	2.5	2.5	2.5	2.5	2.5	2.5	2.5	2.5	2.5	2.6	2.6
Unfunded obligations: past and living generations	2.5	2.4	2.5	2.5	2.5	2.5	2.5	2.5	2.6	2.6	2.7
Unfunded future obligations: living generations	2.5	2.5	2.5	2.5	2.5	2.5	2.5	2.6	2.6	2.6	2.7
Trust fund	0.1	0.1	0.0	0.0	0.0	0.0	0.0	0.0	0.0	0.0	0.0
Unfunded obligations: future generations	0.0	0.0	0.0	0.0	0.0	0.0	0.0	0.0	−0.1	−0.1	−0.1

(d) Medicare supplementary medical insurance (Part B)

	2012	2013	2014	2015	2016	2017	2018	2019	2020	2021	2022
Fiscal imbalance	4.1	4.1	4.1	4.0	4.0	4.0	4.0	4.0	4.0	4.1	4.1
Unfunded obligations: past and living generations	3.1	3.1	3.1	3.1	3.1	3.0	3.1	3.1	3.1	3.1	3.1
Unfunded future obligations: living generations	3.1	3.1	3.1	3.1	3.1	3.1	3.1	3.1	3.2	3.2	3.2
Trust fund	0.0	0.0	0.0	0.0	0.0	0.0	0.0	0.1	0.1	0.1	0.1
Unfunded obligations: future generations	1.0	1.0	1.0	1.0	1.0	1.0	1.0	0.9	0.9	0.9	0.9

(e) Medicare prescription drugs (Part D)

	2012	2013	2014	2015	2016	2017	2018	2019	2020	2021	2022
Fiscal imbalance	3.3	3.3	3.3	3.3	3.3	3.3	3.3	3.3	3.4	3.4	3.4
Unfunded obligations: past and living generations	1.9	1.9	1.9	1.9	1.9	2.0	2.0	2.0	2.1	2.1	2.1
Unfunded future obligations: living generations	1.9	1.9	1.9	1.9	1.9	2.0	2.0	2.0	2.1	2.1	2.1
Trust fund	0.0	0.0	0.0	0.0	0.0	0.0	0.0	0.0	0.0	0.0	0.0
Unfunded obligations: future generations	1.4	1.4	1.4	1.3	1.3	1.3	1.3	1.3	1.3	1.3	1.3

Source: Author's calculations.

imbalance by more would be more 'fiscally responsible' in that it would claw back more of the net benefit to current generations under existing Social Security policies and impose a smaller cost increase on future generations.

Economic effects of the current US federal fiscal stance

Transferring a dollar of resources from someone who consumes relatively little out of each extra dollar they earn to someone else who consumes a lot more is likely to increase total consumption in the economy. The generational imbalance measure reveals the amount of additional resource that today's generations may expect to receive from social insurance programmes over and above their past payroll taxes under current policies. Of course, the expectation of today's younger generations when it comes to receiving pensions and other benefits in the future may be lower than the generational imbalances estimated here because the younger generations may expect current social insurance policies to be changed during their remaining lifetimes. Indeed, the figures shown here suggest that change is inevitable and the longer it is delayed the larger any changes will be. However, older generations, (for example, those aged 55 and older) might expect that they would be protected from future policy adjustments that are designed to reduce fiscal imbalances, at least as far as currently existing social insurance programmes are concerned. The reality of social security reform tends to be that the older generations are protected from the financial effects of policy change. Indeed, given that large-scale reform in the next few years seems unlikely, those over age 55 could reasonably expect to receive the full benefits that have been promised under current policies.

Ultimately, the excess benefits awarded to current generations would have to be paid for out of excess contributions over benefits of future social insurance programme participants. Thus, current social insurance policy paths (as reflected in the CBO's projections) that involve resource transfers from future generations to those alive today are likely to stimulate private consumption spending, reduce private saving and make current national consumption larger than could be financed had current generations been compelled to spend out of their own resources. To-day's boost to consumption spending will be reversed when future generations enter economic life and must pay higher social insurance taxes or tolerate reduced social in-surance benefits to pay for the excess benefits to today's (and past) retirees.

The first row of Table 11 indicates that today's Social Security and Medicare policies will transfer net excess benefits to the tune of $66 trillion from future generations towards current generations. Large additions to the social insurance programmes that involve providing more bene-fits to the early participants have been on-going since the inception of Social Security. These additions included the introduction of Medicare in the mid 1960s; the indexa-tion of Social Security benefits to inflation during the mid 1970s; and the introduction of Medicare prescription drug coverage for older people in 2003. 'Obamacare' has expand-ed health insurance and boosts the inter-generational transfers further by imposing higher health insurance premiums on younger people and future generations relative to their expected health service benefits. This growth in net transfers towards the older generations appears to be the key explanation of why US national saving has declined secularly since the late 1970s from an average of between 9 and 10 per cent of GDP to close to zero during the late 1990s, a level from which it has not recovered.

The transfer of resources to today's older generations will be realised over time as monthly benefit cheques and health care reimbursements are paid out. Nevertheless, the expectation of that resource transfer is likely to influence their current consumption behaviour and would be reflected in current consumption statistics – those nearing and in retirement do not have to save to the same extent to fund their income and health care. Calculations of consumption profiles by age from US micro-data sources throughout the 1990s and 2000s suggest that consumption spending of the older generations has advanced much more rapidly compared with that of younger generations. This is consistent with the belief that older generations are more confident of receiving the benefits of current social security and health care policies.

The lines in Figures 5 and 6 show consumption expenditures per person by age for males and females respectively at different times. The heavier lines are smoothed[9] whereas the lighter lines show actual per capita consumption

---

9   The smoothing is done by fitting a third-order polynomial curve – hence the label 'Poly' for each smoothed curve in the two figures.

Figure 5   **Male consumption by age group**

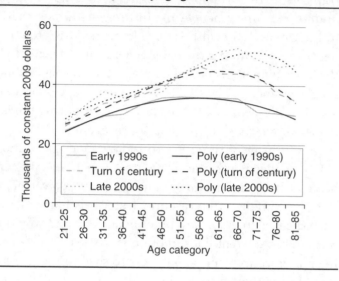

expenditures by age for males and females. The three smoothed profiles represent consumption spending during the early 1990s (shown as the unbroken line), consumption profiles at the turn of the century (shown as dashes) and the consumption profile in the late 2000s (shown as dots). All estimates are in constant 2009 dollars. The figures show a distinctly stronger upward surge in consumption over time by older generations compared with younger ones. Without ongoing inter-generational wealth transfers favouring older generations, we would expect the shift in consumption profiles from gains in wealth to be proportional across the age range. The observed larger increase

Figure 6 **Female consumption by age group**

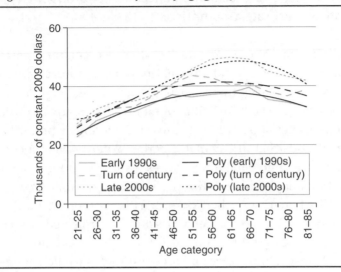

for older generations is consistent with the conjecture of a significant ongoing resource transfer from younger and future generations towards older ones in the US from the operation of social insurance programmes with mandatory nationwide participation.[10]

---

10 There may be other factors that have contributed to the observed faster increases in the consumption of older relative to younger generations. Two obvious ones are a globalisation-induced slowdown in expected future earnings on the part of the young and increased longevity insurance through larger wealth holdings in annuitised form through government programmes and reverse mortgages for the old.

Sensitivity of US fiscal imbalance ratio to productivity and interest rate assumptions

Discounting is the method by which we compare costs today with costs in the future. Discounting future dollars or pounds places them 'on par' with current dollars by allowing for the 'time value of money'. The source of this value is the opportunity to invest for a longer period of time funds that are available earlier. Alternatively, a cost that will come due later requires a smaller fund to be invested today to meet it. The discount rate assumption used here is taken from the CBO's short-term interest rate assumptions for the first ten years and the projected annual long-term interest rate on government debt thereafter.

The fiscal imbalance and other estimates would change under alternative assumptions about the long-term government interest rate and the economy's productivity growth rate. One complaint often made in debates about fiscal imbalances is that the interest rate assumption determines how rapidly the fiscal imbalance (which is similar to a corpus of debt) grows over time. The interest rate assumption also helps determine the size of the fiscal imbalance. It is often suggested that fiscal imbalance calculations are 'artificially high' because interest rates at the moment are unusually low. Calculations are also criticised for being sensitive to the discount rate which, it is argued, does not affect the actual cash flows that will be incurred by the government. Though it is a complex issue, the discount rate is important.

Table 13 **Sensitivity of the fiscal imbalance ratio to variation in long-term interest rates and productivity growth assumptions (baseline projections; percentage of uncapped payrolls)**

CBO baseline projections		Annual productivity growth assumption (%)		
		1.5	**2.0**	**2.5**
Interest rate assumption (%)	**2.4**	13.7	13.4	13.0
	3.2	11.9	11.7	11.5
	4.0	11.0	10.7	10.5
CBO alternative projections				
Interest rate assumption (%)	**2.4**	19.5	20.6	21.4
	3.2	18.5	19.7	20.8
	4.0	18.1	19.1	20.1

Source: Author's calculations.

The productivity growth rate assumption determines how rapidly the economy – and the capacity to pay off debt – grows over time. Under normal economic conditions, the long-term interest rate exceeds the economy's productivity growth rate. In general, the more steeply the projected gap between federal receipts and expenditures increases, the larger the variation in dollar estimates of the fiscal imbalance in response to a variation in the interest rate used to discount annual fiscal shortfalls. However, changes in interest rate and the productivity growth rate also yield roughly proportionate variations in the present values of GDP and payrolls, which constitute the bases for determining the economy's capacity to resolve the fiscal imbalance. Hence, the ratio measure of the fiscal imbalance is more stable than the dollar measure in response to changes in assumed interest rates and productivity growth rates. It can therefore be seen that the criticism of fiscal imbalance measures as being too sensitive to interest rates only really applies to measures that are calculated in dollar terms.

Table 13 shows how ratios of baseline and alternative fiscal imbalances to total present value of payrolls change in response to changes in the interest and productivity growth rate assumptions (we use values 25 per cent higher and lower than the CBO's long-term estimates). The table shows that, under baseline policies, the fiscal imbalance ratio ranges between 11.0 per cent and 13.7 per cent of the total present value of payrolls. Under the alternative policies it ranges between 18.1 per cent and 21.4 per cent. Thus, different assumptions about long-term interest rate and productivity growth rates do not appear to significantly influence the estimated size of fiscal imbalance ratios.

7 FISCAL IMBALANCES IN EU NATIONS: SHORT-TERM METRICS

As has been mentioned earlier, the EU's immediate fiscal and economic crisis has focused policymakers' attention on short-term measures of the fiscal situation. Government revenues and expenditures in the 27 EU countries have been affected by the global economic crisis and by the policy reactions of EU member nations. The ten charts in Figure 7 cover the aggregate of 27 EU nations (in the first chart on the left-hand side) and the nine key EU economies separately. For the EU as a whole, general government revenues and expenditures were almost balanced at about 45 per cent of GDP during the fiscal year 2007. The onset of the recession saw only a slight decline in government revenues. General government expenditure, however, rose sharply after 2007 to exceed 50 per cent of GDP by 2009. The gap between expenditure and revenues narrowed slightly after 2009 to 4.5 per cent of GDP during fiscal year 2011.

The magnitude of the increases in annual deficits in EU member nations depended upon how severely a country's growth was affected by the 2008–9 recession and on the size of bank bailouts and other fiscal measures that were adopted. Among the countries which managed to maintain a better fiscal position, only Germany was able to restrain public expenditure within 50 per cent of GDP. The

Figure 7 **Government revenues and expenditures as a percentage of GDP in selected EU countries**

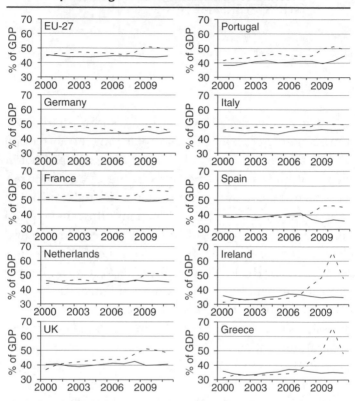

Notes: Unbroken lines show government revenues as a percentage of GDP; dashed lines show government expenditure as a percentage of GDP.
Source: OECD Statistical Extracts.

largest increase in post-recession deficits occurred in the United Kingdom, where the revenue shortfall increased to 11.4 per cent of GDP by 2009. Although it has narrowed since, it still stood at almost 8 per cent of GDP in 2011.

Figure 8 **General government debt as a percentage of annual GDP in selected EU countries: 2007 and 2010**

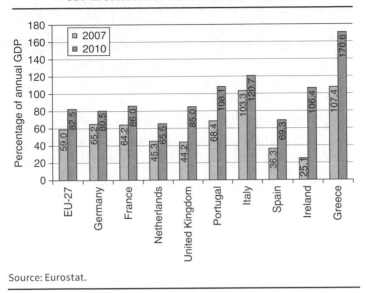

Source: Eurostat.

Portugal, Italy, Spain, Ireland and Greece face serious post-recession fiscal challenges. Of these, Portugal and Italy were running fiscal deficits throughout the 2000s, with deficits increasing sharply during the 2008–9 recession. Note, however, that Italy's general government expenditures have declined since 2009 as a result of budget consolidation measures. The revenue shortfall in Italy was smaller because of the effect of fiscal consolidations and revenue increases from 2005.

Figure 8 illustrates the size of government debt (as a percentage of then current GDP) for the EU-27 and for each of the nine selected EU nations before the onset of the global recession in 2007 and again in 2010. As expected, government debt as a percentage of GDP has increased in the 27 EU nations as a whole and in the member nations shown in the figure. In the EU-27 countries, debt shot up from less than 60 per cent of EU-27 GDP to slightly more than 80 per cent. Among fiscally stronger and larger nations, German, French and British debt increased to around 80 per cent of GDP. The Netherlands' 2011 debt ratio of 65.5 per cent, however, remained close to the 60 per cent threshold specified under the European Stability and Growth Pact (SGP).

8 BACKGROUND TO THE EU'S LONG-TERM FISCAL POSITION

As has been discussed, the fiscal imbalance measure is a forward-looking, long-term budget metric that measures the size, in present discounted value terms, of the government's future unfunded obligations under the assumption that current fiscal laws and practices will be maintained throughout the projection horizon. It is the sum of explicit debt inherited from the past and the present value of future shortfalls of projected government receipts raised to finance spending. The measure indicates the impact of baby boomers retiring and national budgets becoming more heavily weighted towards providing pensions and social protection services.

The fiscal imbalance measure therefore provides policy-relevant information about future fiscal reform alternatives that could be employed to improve or maintain sustainable fiscal policies. It also allows us to understand how different underlying factors contribute to the baseline 2010 fiscal imbalances in different EU nations.

The first of these factors is population ageing. The retirement of the baby boomers and their replacement in EU nations' workforces by relatively smaller birth cohorts is resulting in a declining ratio of working-age to retired individuals. Figure 9 shows projected declines in the

Figure 9 **Worker-to-retiree population ratios in selected EU nations**

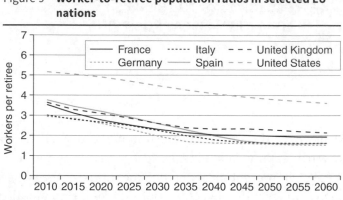

Source: Calculated using United States' Social Security Administration and Eurostat data.

worker-to-retiree ratios in five major EU countries and the US for comparison. For most of the EU countries shown, this ratio currently stands at between three and four workers per retiree but, for most, it is projected to decline to below two workers per retiree by the middle of this century. The projected ratio also declines for the US, but it will remain considerably above those in the major EU nations.

The second factor is budget structure. Important issues here include the distribution of taxes and benefits across individuals by age and gender and the share of the budget distributed to programmes that involve inter-generational redistribution on the one hand versus the share used to provide pure public goods on the other hand. The latter group of programmes includes external defence and judicial and legislative functions where the benefits accrue to the entire citizenry – those alive today and future

Figure 10 **Social protection expenditure shares in GDP (2010)**

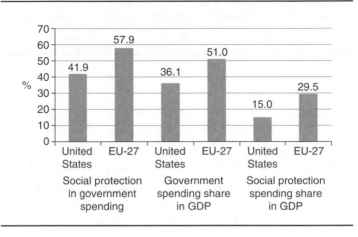

generations. The former group of programmes includes social protection and public pension programmes.

It's worth comparing the budget structures of EU nations as a whole with that of the United States. Figure 10 shows that the share of social protection expenditures in government spending, and the share of government spending in GDP are both significantly larger in the EU compared with the US. The US spends just one half as much (15 per cent) of its GDP on social protection expenditures as the EU (29.5 per cent). To the extent that EU expenditure on social protection is directed toward retirees, the on-going demographic transition in the EU is projected to generate a larger surge in government expenditures under current policies than it will in the US. The worker-to-retiree ratio will be much lower in the EU and, in addition, the pattern of spending is such that overall government spending is more sensitive to demographic change. This means that future structural budget imbalances are likely to worsen more in EU nations than in the US. In turn, this means that the fiscal imbalance metric (described and calculated below) is likely to be larger among EU nations than in the US.

Retirement support programmes are an important subset of social protection programmes. While social protection encompasses all economic contingencies and misfortunes that may befall people of all ages, retirement support programmes target support towards retirees and are financed out of taxes paid by working generations. Figure 10 shows two sets of stylised profiles of taxes and transfers by age and gender that characterise financing and benefit disbursement under most public pension programmes.

The two charts in Figure 11 show index values of average social protection receipts (benefits) and average social insurance contributions (taxes) relative to the average value for a 40-year-old male. The two charts show that while benefits are heavily concentrated on older individuals (retirees receive much more per €1.0 received by 40-year-old males) the contributions are taken more or less exclusively from working-age individuals. The larger the share of budgetary resources devoted to such transfer programmes, the more heavily is the budget structure oriented toward inter-generational resource redistributions.

Today, 47.3 per cent of the US federal budget and 54.2 per cent of the average budget of EU countries is devoted to programmes that primarily benefit retirees. The retirement of the baby-boomers and slowing growth of the

Figure 11 **Relative profiles of social protection expenditures and social insurance contributions (index 40-year-old male = 1)**

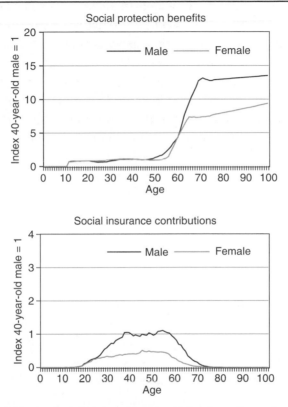

Source: Author's calculations based on micro-data information on the European Union's Income and Living Conditions Survey.

working-age population will impose growing pressures on those countries' budgets during coming decades. Isolating the contribution of these budget structures, both in terms of the share of the budget devoted to retirement programmes and the age distribution of taxes and benefits, reveals how much of a particular nation's fiscal imbalance arises because its budget structure is more heavily weighted toward retirement programmes than the average budget structure in EU countries taken as a whole. The calculations in the following chapters demonstrate, firstly, that the long-term fiscal position in the EU on average is worse than that in the US but that, secondly, there are huge variations within the European Union countries.

9 POLICY ERRORS ARISING FROM SHORT-TERM FISCAL MEASURES

Despite the importance of long-term, forward-looking fiscal imbalance measures, policy in EU countries is still dictated by shorter-term and backward-looking measures. The continuing recessionary environment has negatively affected the long-term fiscal picture in most EU countries. Fiscal imbalance estimates computed in 2006 (with a base year of 2004) suggested that the sum of explicit debt and implicit future unfunded obligations of EU nations under then current policies created a shortfall equivalent to 8.3 per cent of the present value of GDP, on average, for the then 25 EU nations (EU-25).[1] That estimate implies that EU nations would, on average, have to set aside 8.3 per cent of EU's annual GDP in order to resolve the shortfall of prospective revenues relative to government spending under their (then) current fiscal policies.

However, the 2008–9 recession reduced revenue growth in some EU countries and induced significantly larger expenditures in most countries on social protection and other government programmes. Economic growth projections

---

1   See 'Measuring the Unfunded Obligations of European Nations', National Center for Policy Analysis, Policy Report 319, January 2009.

have been scaled back by international agencies such as the International Monetary Fund, implying that the urgency of dealing with long-term imbalances through politically difficult policy reforms has increased.[2] As we will see in the next chapter, this has led to a large increase in long-term fiscal imbalances. However, policy is still based on measures focused on short-term debt and budget deficits.

For example, the European Stability and Growth Pact specifies deficit and debt limits: 3 per cent and 60 per cent of annual GDP respectively. Euro zone countries are supposed to adhere to this constraint in order to facilitate sound monetary policy and avoid the excessive negative spillover costs on other countries that would emerge if some member nations were to deficit-finance considerably larger amounts of their domestic public expenditures.

As Figure 8 shows, explicit debt levels far exceeded 60 per cent in many EU nations in 2011.[3] However, focusing policy on returning to those levels is mistaken because explicit debt levels do not fully reveal the extent of policy reforms needed or, indeed, which policies should be targeted to ensure long-term fiscal stability. Explicit debt measures information about in-built deficit and debt implications

---

2 See World Economic Outlook, International Monetary Fund, October 2012. The report states that: 'The problem of high public debt existed before the Great Recession, because of population aging and growth in entitlement spending, but the crisis brought the need to address it forward from the long to the medium term'.

3 EMU countries with 2011 debt levels within the Stability and Growth Pact limits include Estonia, Luxembourg, Slovenia, Slovakia and Finland.

of today's policies given each nation's future demographic and economic profile. Indeed, fiscal policy targeting based on such metrics may divert policymakers' attention away from longer-term structural budget problems lurking within current tax and expenditure programmes. Artificial mechanisms can be used – as indeed they have been used – to reduce current deficits even though they may have detrimental effects in the long term. This could lead to biases and delays in implementing the fiscal adjustments needed to adequately meet the population's future needs for public goods and services and to achieve true prospective economic convergence.

This problem of inappropriate metrics leading to poor policy seems particularly acute in the EU. Indeed, it is worth noting that in two non-euro zone countries – Poland and Hungary – the government has taken ownership of private pension funds to reduce explicit government debt while making future state pension commitments to the affected groups. A proper inter-generational accounting measure would not suggest that this policy was beneficial because it would have counted in government debt the future pension liabilities and that increase in government debt would have cancelled out the assets taken by the government. Although the motivation was different, a similar situation occurred in the UK when the government took the assets of the Royal Mail pension fund and gave the workers promises of government pensions in return. Again, the explicit government debt was reduced but future government liabilities – in this case contractual – were increased.

A forward-oriented fiscal policy measure – the fiscal imbalance – takes account of the implications of current policies on the government's prospective finances. As it is calculated as a present value measure, like a body of debt, it grows larger over time by accruing interest except when the initial fiscal imbalance happens to be exactly zero.[4] The advantage of calculating country-specific fiscal imbalances is that it enables exploration of policy alternatives such as how much a particular tax base would need to be tapped, how much particular expenditures must be reduced, and so on in order to achieve long-term budget balance. Moreover, potential policy changes to restore prospective budget balance can be decomposed into tax increases or benefit reductions per person by age and gender to explore the distributional trade-offs involved. Because of its focus on prospective fiscal outcomes under current policies given a nation's demographic and economic profile, complementing stability and growth pact deficit and debt rules with fiscal imbalance measures would show member nation's fiscal stances more clearly and comprehensively. It would also enable EU policymakers to tailor convergence criteria and strategies to each nation's prospective demographic and economic environments and constraints, including budget structures and inter-generational transfers being implemented through alternative social protection and pension programmes. These benefits, of course, would

---

4 This property of the fiscal imbalance measure motivates the term 'fiscal imbalance' as opposed to 'fiscal gap'. The property is described in greater detail in Gokhale and Smetters (2003).

not only accrue to euro zone countries but to those countries that operated independent monetary policies such as
the UK. However, these measures are especially relevant
in EU euro zone countries given the role of supranational
bodies in setting the overall constraints for national fiscal
management.

10 HOW BIG ARE EU FISCAL IMBALANCES?

The fiscal imbalances of 25 EU countries that are reported below take into account age- and gender-specific taxes and expenditures obtained from the European Union Income and Living Conditions micro-data survey. The tax categories distributed by age and gender include labour and capital income taxes, social insurance contributions and consumption taxes. The spending categories distributed by age and gender according to micro-data relative profiles include housing and community services, health, education and social protection expenditures. Other 'pure public good' provisions such as defence, environmental protection, public order and safety, other economic affairs interventions and general public services are assumed to be distributed equally per person by age and gender as these expenditure items benefit the general citizenry (including future generations).

Fiscal imbalance estimates are constructed for each EU nation using Eurostat's demographic and budget projections. General government revenues and expenditures projected through 2060 are discounted using an inflation-adjusted interest rate of 2.5 per cent.[1] Future real

---

1 This real annual discount rate is calculated by subtracting long-term inflation expectations of 2.0 per cent per year from the yield on 30-year bonds of 4.54 per cent. Both statistics are taken from

expenditures and taxes are assumed to grow at EU-country-specific historical average labour productivity growth rates. Generally, older EU nations such as Italy, Spain, Denmark and France experienced slower economic growth during the 2000s compared with newer ones such as Estonia, Latvia, Poland and Slovakia. EU-wide labour productivity growth during the last decade averaged 1.5 per cent per year. It is worth noting, however, that government expenditures are particularly high during recession years because of automatic increases in social protection benefits and special fiscal stimulus policies that various countries have adopted. To correct for this and obtain a 'structural expenditure baseline', base year 2010 expenditures are reduced across the board using the difference between average expenditures as a share of GDP during 2000–10 and 2010 expenditures as a share of 2010 GDP. This adjustment reduces expenditures per capita in 2010, and, hence, growth-adjusted expenditures in future years and correspondingly reduces fiscal imbalance estimates. The fiscal imbalances calculated after making this adjustment, if positive, are interpreted as structural budget imbalances that would need to be addressed by additional future policy changes. This adjustment is clearly an approximation. In some countries, such as the UK, there were rapid increases in structural spending during the period 2000–10 so the average of spending levels during that decade will

Eurostat. This discount rate is only slightly different from that used in the earlier version of this study: 2.4 per cent per year. See 'Measuring the Unfunded Obligations of European Nations,' National Center for Policy Analysis, Policy Report 319, January 2009.

understate structural spending level in 2010 itself. For other countries, the opposite may apply. A similar adjustment is not implemented for revenues because, as Figure 7 suggests, EU revenues were not significantly different during the 2008–9 recessionary period compared with their average during the 2000s.

In the earlier chapters, there was detailed discussion of the potential fiscal scenarios in the US. The different EU countries have, of course, reacted very differently to the fiscal problems caused by recent events. Some countries are cutting expenditure programmes. A number of countries are also planning future cuts in entitlements, for example, by raising the pension age. The projections of the long-term fiscal position do not take into account policies which are planned but are yet to be implemented – whether these are favourable or unfavourable – even if such changes have been announced. The reason for this is that, even when policy changes have been announced, their implementation is uncertain. If we take the UK as an example, some of the fiscal adjustment revealed as necessary in the analysis below may well arise as a result of increases in state pension age that the government has already announced but not yet implemented. The government plans to increase the state pension age to 68 by 2046 and then, possibly, link it to longevity. It is likely that these reforms will be accelerated. At the same time, it is conceivable that these reforms may be scaled back by future governments.[2] If this reform

2 Recall, for example, French President François Hollande's decision to roll back the national retirement age to 60 in 2012, just two years after President Sarkozy had increased it to 62.

Figure 12 **Fiscal imbalance as of 2010 (explicit and implicit debt) as a percentage of the present value of GDP**

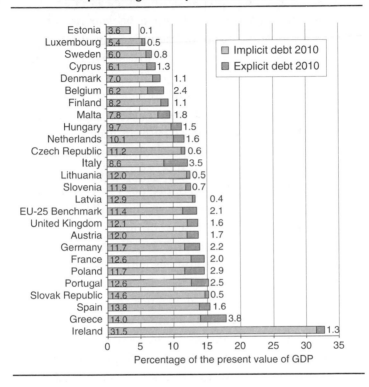

Percentage of the present value of GDP

– and other related reforms – is implemented, it will reduce the 'work' that has to be done by other adjustments to taxes and future spending commitments to eliminate the fiscal imbalance.

Figure 12 shows fiscal imbalance estimates for 25 out of the 27 EU member nations – those for which all of the required demographic and budget information was available. The countries are listed in Figure 12 according to the size of their overall fiscal imbalance as a percentage of the present value of their GDP. As is clear from the figure, most countries' explicit debt inherited from the past (shaded in dark grey on the rightmost end of the horizontal bars) comprises a very small portion of their total fiscal imbalance, which is the sum of implicit and explicit debt. Implicit debt – the present discounted value of prospective (structural) budget shortfalls (the light grey parts of the horizontal bars) – makes up the overwhelming portion of fiscal imbalances of all EU nations.

At 32.8 per cent of the present value of its GDP, Ireland's fiscal imbalance is by far the largest among all EU countries. Greece, Spain, the Slovak Republic and Portugal follow with fiscal imbalances exceeding 15 per cent in each case. Those are followed by 13 countries with fiscal imbalances between 10.0 and 15.0 per cent. Among these, Poland's fiscal imbalance is estimated at 14.6 per cent and Hungary's at 11.3 per cent. France and Germany are also among this group, with fiscal imbalances of 14.6 and 13.9 per cent respectively. At 13.6 per cent, the UK's fiscal imabalance is very close to the EU-wide average of 13.5 per cent.[3] A group of eight countries that includes Finland, Belgium, Denmark and Sweden has fiscal imbalances below 10 per cent of GDP. Estonia has the smallest fiscal imbalance of 3.7 per cent among the 25 EU countries considered here.

Note that even a 5 per cent imbalance is quite large as it implies the need to surrender an additional 5 per cent

---

3   The numbers cited in the text may not add up exactly to the components shown in the figures and tables because of rounding errors.

of GDP each and every year in the future to fund existing government spending plans given planned taxation levels under current fiscal laws and practices.[4] Thus, a fiscal imbalance of 13.5 per cent on average across the 25 EU countries considered here represents a huge structural divergence between prospective government expenditures and revenues driven by demographic factors (the ageing of the EU baby-boomers combined with low and declining mortality, low fertility and low external net immigration rates).

Is it plausible that projections of future general government revenues and expenditures would yield an imbalance of 13.5 per cent for the EU as a whole? One can examine this by considering that the fiscal imbalance is simply the discounted sum of future annual budget shortfalls under the assumption that both will be governed by projected demographic changes combined with today's fiscal policies. Current policies resulted in an annual budget structural shortfall of 5.2 per cent of GDP in 2010.[5] However,

---

4   Such large fiscal policy changes are very rare. One very large, and frequently discussed, fiscal transfer policy involved the sacrifice of about 5 per cent of GDP by the residents of then West Germany to finance German reunification. This was regarded as an enormous fiscal transfer but that reallocation lasted for a finite time period and therefore amounted to much less than 5 per cent of the present value of all future GDP. Almost all other major historical episodes, including major wars, involved discrete fiscal resource reallocations that have been far smaller than 5 per cent of the present value of GDP.

5   The 2010 EU-25 deficit reported in Eurostat equals 6 per cent of 2010 GDP. However, the adjustment described earlier to obtain a 'structural expenditure baseline' reduces it to around 5 per cent of GDP.

population ageing increases projected budget imbalances at a faster rate than GDP growth because of the growing gap between tax revenues and benefit payments, health costs and other budget items associated with an ageing population. The result is that on current policies EU-wide annual general government budget deficits increase in future years: the annual structural deficit-to-GDP ratio will increase to 7.8 per cent by 2020 on current policies, 11.4 per cent by 2030, 14.3 per cent by 2040, 16.1 per cent by 2050 and 16.3 per cent by 2060. The overall fiscal imbalance ratio – which is just the ratio of the present value of annual budget shortfalls to the present value of projected GDP – turns out to be 13.5 per cent for the EU-25 group of nations. This sense check of looking at the future fiscal problems caused by ageing populations, combined with a pre-existing budget deficit, suggests that the numbers here are an accurate projection of the future implications of current EU fiscal policies.

As discussed below, such a large EU-wide fiscal imbalance implies the need for quite significant tax increases or expenditure cuts as a percentage of those respective bases: worker earnings and retirement and health benefits. Most EU nations will have to undergo significant future fiscal adjustments to cover projected government expenditures or to contain them within the revenues that will be available under current policies. Of course, there are a number of ways to bridge the gap. There could be tax increases and/ or expenditure cuts of various sizes and duration. A few of the alternatives are described below for the 25 EU nations analysed.

Alternative policy actions

EU residents' private final consumption rate is about 58.1 per cent of GDP on average. This means that a 13.5 per cent fiscal imbalance as a share of GDP translates into a 23.2 percentage point increase in the consumption tax rate – however it is operationalised.[1] Alternatively, since employee compensation averages 49.6 per cent of GDP across all EU nations, the average tax rate on employee compensation would have to be increased by 27.2 percentage points, on average, in EU countries.[2] Another way to raise the required resources would be through reductions in government expenditure. For example, across the EU as a whole, health

---

1   For example, it could occur through a value added tax, a tax on final sales or other consumption taxes. This increase is necessary after adjusting the rates appropriately to compensate for exclusions and deductions that change the underlying consumption tax base. The estimate of the share of private consumption in GDP is calculated from Eurostat data for 2011 as equal to total final consumption spending minus government final consumption spending divided by GDP.

2   The share of employee compensation in GDP is calculated from Eurostat information on GDP and its main components. The nominal aggregates for GDP (at market prices) and employee compensation are summed across EU-25 nations. The ratio of employee compensation to GDP equals 49.6 per cent.

plus social protection expenditures would have to be reduced by about 48.7 per cent. All of these changes would have to be implemented immediately and maintained permanently in order to fully resolve the fiscal imbalance. These and other policy alternatives are shown in Table 14 in the row labelled 'EU-25 benchmark' (shaded in grey).

The policy changes that are reported here as necessary to balance the government's books in the long term should not be interpreted as forecasts. Rather, they are alternative characterisations of the structural imbalance built into current EU fiscal policies, on average, as of 2010 – the base year for the calculations. Table 14 also shows the country-specific tax increases and benefit cuts that would be necessary under alternative ways of resolving each country's fiscal imbalance. The required increases in EU countries' total general government revenues range from 9.0 per cent for Estonia to 92.9 per cent for Ireland – as shown in the last column of Table 14. Alternatively, required total government expenditure cuts range from 9.1 per cent in Estonia to 50.1 per cent in Ireland. Among large EU nations (Germany, France, the UK, Italy and Spain), fiscal consolidations to eliminate the imbalance would require elimination of about one third of total government expenditures (ranging from 24.1 per cent in Italy to 33.1 per cent in Spain).

It is worth reflecting on the meaning of these figures. The figure for required expenditure cuts in the UK suggests that more than one quarter of government expenditure would have to be cut in the long run out of projections based on existing expenditure levels. This is a very large

Table 14 **Percentage point increases in average tax rates and percentage point cuts to selected expenditure programmes needed – immediately and permanently – to eliminate fiscal imbalances in EU countries**

Country	Final consumption	Labour compensation	Health and social protection expenditures	Total general government expenditures	Total general government taxes
	Percentage point increases in average tax rates on tax base specified in column label		Alternative percentage cuts in expenditures or increases in general government taxes		
Ireland	66.4	74.2	130.9	50.1	92.9
Greece	24.2	49.1	68.3	34.6	43.4
Spain	26.6	31.2	64.9	33.1	41.1
Slovak Republic	26.0	40.1	81.5	38.0	46.6
Portugal	23.0	30.2	61.2	29.4	36.1
Poland	23.8	39.5	66.6	32.0	38.5
France	25.1	27.3	45.4	25.7	29.0
Germany	24.2	27.4	50.3	29.1	31.6
Austria	24.9	27.4	45.7	25.9	28.2
United Kingdom	21.1	25.3	52.8	27.4	33.9
EU-25 benchmark	23.2	27.2	48.7	26.3	29.9
Latvia	21.0	31.3	74.1	30.6	37.3
Slovenia	22.1	23.5	49.3	25.0	28.0
Lithuania	19.5	30.3	63.1	30.8	37.0
Italy	20.0	28.6	43.4	24.1	26.1
Czech Republic	23.3	28.1	55.1	26.9	29.9
Netherlands	25.5	22.8	45.5	22.7	24.8
Hungary	21.2	24.9	49.1	22.6	24.3
Malta	15.8	21.7	48.9	23.1	24.8
Finland	16.8	18.1	29.2	16.7	17.5
Belgium	16.4	16.9	32.0	16.5	17.3
Denmark	16.7	14.6	24.2	14.1	14.7
Cyprus	11.2	16.3	49.7	16.1	18.1
Sweden	14.2	12.9	24.0	13.1	13.1
Luxembourg	18.1	12.3	24.7	13.5	13.7
Estonia	7.0	7.6	18.5	9.1	9.0

Source: Author's calculations based on Eurostat and European Union Income and Living Conditions Survey.

123

required adjustment: it takes into account not just the fact that all government spending was not financed by existing taxes in the base year – the government was borrowing around 8 per cent of GDP, roughly equivalent to 20–25 per cent of government spending – but also that, as the population ages, the tax base will decline relative to projected expenditures, especially on health, pensions and social care given current policies. If there is no change in policy, the gap between tax revenues and spending will naturally rise as a result of population ageing.

Although the only way to resolve the fiscal imbalance is through future expenditure and tax policy changes, there are various ways in which such changes could be introduced. For example, pension age could be raised; pensions could be 'under-indexed'; health care financed by the state could be provided more cost effectively; or co-payments could be required for health care.

Although the estimates are expressed in terms of the present value of all future GDP, it could be argued that future generations may be better able to bear the costs of adjustment if national output increases faster. However, if the gap is closed by raising taxes, it is likely that GDP growth rates could themselves fall, especially given the already high level of taxes in most EU countries. Indeed, it is suggested below that increased national income growth will not occur unless the government deals with its long-term fiscal problems.

The problems of delaying policy action

In the future, fiscal imbalances may continue to increase. They will certainly grow larger if policymakers delay implementing policy adjustments because they will accrue interest costs at a faster rate than the economy's productivity growth rate. Far from going away if ignored, fiscal imbalances will grow bigger.

That this is true for almost all EU countries is shown in Table 15. This table shows the time profile of fiscal imbalances as a share of the present value of GDP calculated over rolling 51-year spans beginning with 2010–60 and ending with 2016–66 (column headers show the first or base year of each 51-year time span). For all EU nations, fiscal imbalance ratios calculated over successive 51-year horizons increase over time. The simple reason for this is that the sum of an additional year's fiscal shortfall plus interest cost accrual on the existing shortfall in the ratio's numerator outpaces the change in the present value of GDP from shifting the time frame forward by one year. This happens because, apart from the addition of one year's deficit at the outer end of the projection window, GDP growth is generally slower than interest cost accruals on the initial fiscal imbalance. For example, the UK's fiscal imbalance ratio would increase from 13.6 per cent of the present value of GDP to almost 17.1 per cent by 2016 if no policy adjustments are made until that year. Table 15 shows that roughly 55 per cent of this change arises from interest accrual on the fiscal imbalance and about 45 per cent arises from the forward shift in the projection window.

Table 15 Projected annual changes in fiscal imbalances: interest accruals and shifting the projection window

Country	Measure	Per cent of present value of GDP						
		2010	2011	2012	2013	2014	2015	2016
EU-25 Benchmark	Fiscal imbalance	13.49	14.02	14.57	15.13	15.71	16.31	16.92
	Annual change	—	0.21	0.22	0.22	0.22	0.22	0.23
	Interest accrual	—	0.13	0.13	0.14	0.14	0.14	0.15
	Shift in projection window	—	0.09	0.08	0.08	0.08	0.08	0.08
Belgium	Fiscal imbalance	8.67	8.95	9.24	9.53	9.83	10.13	10.43
	Annual change	—	0.13	0.13	0.13	0.13	0.13	0.13
	Interest accrual	—	0.08	0.09	0.09	0.09	0.09	0.09
	Shift in projection window	—	0.05	0.04	0.04	0.04	0.04	0.04
Czech Republic	Fiscal imbalance	11.79	12.44	13.13	13.84	14.58	15.34	16.14
	Annual change	—	0.42	0.42	0.43	0.43	0.43	0.43
	Interest accrual	—	0.19	0.19	0.19	0.20	0.20	0.21
	Shift in projection window	—	0.24	0.23	0.23	0.23	0.23	0.22
Denmark	Fiscal imbalance	8.15	8.47	8.79	9.12	9.47	9.82	10.18
	Annual change	—	0.13	0.13	0.13	0.13	0.13	0.14
	Interest accrual	—	0.08	0.08	0.08	0.08	0.08	0.09
	Shift in projection window	—	0.05	0.05	0.05	0.05	0.05	0.05
Germany	Fiscal imbalance	13.91	14.51	15.13	15.77	16.43	17.11	17.82
	Annual change	—	0.20	0.21	0.21	0.21	0.21	0.21
	Interest accrual	—	0.13	0.13	0.13	0.14	0.14	0.14
	Shift in projection window	—	0.08	0.08	0.07	0.07	0.07	0.07

Table 15 **Continued**

Country	Measure	Per cent of present value of GDP						
		2010	2011	2012	2013	2014	2015	2016
Estonia	Fiscal imbalance	3.67	3.99	4.33	4.68	5.05	5.45	5.86
	Annual change	—	0.21	0.21	0.21	0.22	0.22	0.22
	Interest accrual	—	0.06	0.07	0.07	0.07	0.07	0.08
	Shift in projection window	—	0.15	0.15	0.15	0.14	0.14	0.14
Ireland	Fiscal imbalance	32.78	34.25	35.79	37.38	39.03	40.74	42.52
	Annual change	—	1.17	1.17	1.18	1.19	1.20	1.20
	Interest accrual	—	0.57	0.58	0.59	0.60	0.61	0.61
	Shift in projection window	—	0.60	0.59	0.59	0.59	0.59	0.58
Greece	Fiscal imbalance	17.79	18.46	19.14	19.84	20.55	21.29	22.04
	Annual change	—	0.27	0.27	0.28	0.28	0.28	0.29
	Interest accrual	—	0.17	0.17	0.18	0.18	0.19	0.19
	Shift in projection window	—	0.10	0.10	0.10	0.10	0.10	0.10
Spain	Fiscal imbalance	15.37	15.98	16.61	17.26	17.92	18.60	19.30
	Annual change	—	0.26	0.26	0.26	0.27	0.27	0.27
	Interest accrual	—	0.15	0.15	0.16	0.16	0.17	0.17
	Shift in projection window	—	0.11	0.11	0.11	0.11	0.11	0.10
France	Fiscal imbalance	14.55	15.10	15.66	16.24	16.83	17.43	18.05
	Annual change	—	0.25	0.25	0.26	0.26	0.26	0.26
	Interest accrual	—	0.15	0.15	0.16	0.16	0.16	0.17
	Shift in projection window	—	0.10	0.10	0.10	0.10	0.10	0.10

Table 15 **Continued**

Country	Measure	Per cent of present value of GDP						
		2010	2011	2012	2013	2014	2015	2016
Italy	Fiscal imbalance	12.15	12.57	12.99	13.43	13.88	14.33	14.80
	Annual change	—	0.15	0.15	0.16	0.16	0.16	0.16
	Interest accrual	—	0.10	0.11	0.11	0.11	0.11	0.12
	Shift in projection window	—	0.05	0.05	0.05	0.05	0.05	0.05
Cyprus	Fiscal imbalance	7.44	7.72	7.99	8.28	8.57	8.86	9.17
	Annual change	—	0.16	0.16	0.16	0.16	0.17	0.17
	Interest accrual	—	0.09	0.09	0.09	0.09	0.09	0.10
	Shift in projection window	—	0.07	0.07	0.07	0.07	0.07	0.07
Latvia	Fiscal imbalance	13.27	14.35	15.50	16.74	18.06	19.47	20.99
	Annual change	—	0.98	0.99	0.99	0.99	1.00	1.00
	Interest accrual	—	0.34	0.34	0.35	0.36	0.36	0.37
	Shift in projection window	—	0.65	0.64	0.64	0.64	0.64	0.63
Lithuania	Fiscal imbalance	12.52	13.53	14.63	15.83	17.13	18.55	20.11
	Annual change	—	0.58	0.59	0.60	0.61	0.62	0.63
	Interest accrual	—	0.22	0.22	0.23	0.23	0.24	0.25
	Shift in projection window	—	0.36	0.37	0.37	0.37	0.38	0.38
Luxembourg	Fiscal imbalance	5.88	6.11	6.34	6.57	6.81	7.05	7.30
	Annual change	—	0.12	0.12	0.12	0.12	0.12	0.12
	Interest accrual	—	0.06	0.06	0.06	0.07	0.07	0.07
	Shift in projection window	—	0.06	0.06	0.06	0.05	0.05	0.05

Table 15 **Continued**

Country	Measure	Per cent of present value of GDP						
		2010	2011	2012	2013	2014	2015	2016
Hungary	Fiscal imbalance	11.28	11.92	12.59	13.30	14.03	14.81	15.61
	Annual change	—	0.31	0.32	0.32	0.33	0.33	0.33
	Interest accrual	—	0.14	0.15	0.15	0.16	0.16	0.16
	Shift in projection window	—	0.17	0.17	0.17	0.17	0.17	0.17
Malta	Fiscal imbalance	9.58	9.98	10.40	10.83	11.27	11.73	12.21
	Annual change	—	0.15	0.15	0.16	0.16	0.16	0.17
	Interest accrual	—	0.09	0.09	0.09	0.10	0.10	0.10
	Shift in projection window	—	0.06	0.06	0.06	0.06	0.07	0.07
The Netherlands	Fiscal imbalance	11.67	12.12	12.59	13.07	13.57	14.08	14.61
	Annual change	—	0.18	0.19	0.19	0.19	0.19	0.19
	Interest accrual	—	0.11	0.12	0.12	0.12	0.12	0.13
	Shift in projection window	—	0.07	0.07	0.07	0.07	0.07	0.07
Austria	Fiscal imbalance	13.70	14.29	14.89	15.51	16.16	16.82	17.51
	Annual change	—	0.26	0.26	0.27	0.27	0.27	0.27
	Interest accrual	—	0.15	0.15	0.15	0.16	0.16	0.16
	Shift in projection window	—	0.12	0.11	0.11	0.11	0.11	0.11
Poland	Fiscal imbalance	14.56	15.01	15.48	15.96	16.45	16.96	17.48
	Annual change	—	0.09	0.09	0.10	0.10	0.10	0.11
	Interest accrual	—	0.07	0.08	0.08	0.08	0.09	0.09
	Shift in projection window	—	0.02	0.02	0.02	0.02	0.02	0.02

Table 15 **Continued**

Country	Measure	Per cent of present value of GDP						
		2010	2011	2012	2013	2014	2015	2016
Portugal	Fiscal imbalance	15.16	15.75	16.37	17.00	17.66	18.33	19.02
	Annual change	—	0.22	0.23	0.23	0.23	0.24	0.24
	Interest accrual	—	0.14	0.14	0.15	0.15	0.15	0.16
	Shift in projection window	—	0.08	0.08	0.08	0.08	0.08	0.08
Slovenia	Fiscal imbalance	12.60	13.27	13.97	14.69	15.44	16.22	17.04
	Annual change	—	0.35	0.35	0.35	0.35	0.35	0.35
	Interest accrual	—	0.16	0.17	0.17	0.17	0.18	0.18
	Shift in projection window	—	0.18	0.18	0.18	0.18	0.17	0.17
Slovakia	Fiscal imbalance	15.17	16.11	17.09	18.12	19.20	20.34	21.53
	Annual change	—	0.66	0.66	0.66	0.66	0.66	0.66
	Interest accrual	—	0.27	0.28	0.28	0.29	0.29	0.29
	Shift in projection window	—	0.39	0.39	0.38	0.38	0.37	0.37
Finland	Fiscal imbalance	9.34	9.72	10.12	10.54	10.96	11.40	11.85
	Annual change	—	0.18	0.18	0.18	0.18	0.18	0.18
	Interest accrual	—	0.10	0.10	0.11	0.11	0.11	0.11
	Shift in projection window	—	0.08	0.08	0.07	0.07	0.07	0.07
Sweden	Fiscal imbalance	6.86	7.16	7.46	7.76	8.07	8.39	8.72
	Annual change	—	0.16	0.16	0.16	0.16	0.16	0.16
	Interest accrual	—	0.08	0.08	0.09	0.09	0.09	0.09
	Shift in projection window	—	0.08	0.07	0.07	0.07	0.07	0.07
UK	Fiscal imbalance	13.64	14.17	14.72	15.28	15.86	16.45	17.06
	Annual change	—	0.30	0.30	0.30	0.30	0.30	0.31
	Interest accrual	—	0.17	0.17	0.17	0.18	0.18	0.18
	Shift in projection window	—	0.13	0.13	0.13	0.13	0.13	0.13

Short-term focus of current budget policy

Although the time window available for EU nations to undertake corrective fiscal adjustments before the problem becomes insurmountable is unknown, EU nations' large and growing fiscal imbalances imply that the window is limited. Growing fiscal imbalances imply that, without corrective action, future implicit budget shortfalls will become explicit, eventually generating significant negative financial market and economic outcomes. Such outcomes – capital flight and sharply rising interest rates – would make it considerably more difficult for EU governments to meet payment commitments to creditors and pay benefits to retirees and other vulnerable groups.

One of the reasons for the lack of progress in making timely adjustments may be the need to focus on short-term fiscal emergencies arising from the recent recession. A case in point is the periodic debt-limit crises in the US that create political froth over short-term debt-limit increases and government funding – which may be distracting policymakers from spending time on carefully crafted fiscal reforms to place government finances on a sustainable course. Another factor is the exclusive focus on short-term and backward-looking metrics such as cash-flow deficits and national debt levels. The euro zone is a case in point as such metrics are enshrined as economic convergence criteria for joining and remaining in the European Monetary Union. One way of understanding why that approach is inadequate is to consider that the addition of the current year's cash-flow shortfall (annual deficit) to the national debt understates the true increase in a nation's indebtedness. The interest cost accrual on the fiscal imbalance, as it comes closer to the time when prospective budget shortfalls must be covered through additional borrowing, adds to the total level of the nation's indebtedness, but this increment is excluded from the standard cash-flow measure of the deficit. Furthermore, future spending commitments exceeding projected revenues are also excluded from backward-looking measures of the total debt.

A key implication of these observations is that the beliefs expressed by some analysts and policymakers – that future economic growth will 'bail us out' from debt overhangs – is misplaced. Uncertainty about how public indebtedness will be resolved appears to be hampering private sector investment and job creation in Europe and the US – witness the large cash hoards within banks and private companies that their managers are unwilling to commit to risky investments. Reorienting government tax and spending policies to significantly resolve the debt overhang – by paring government commitments on social and other spending and eliminating targeted tax preferences to particular voter constituencies – would increase investor confidence in the prospective sustainability and stability of the fiscal and economic environment. It appears more sensible, then, to think about the causality in reverse order: rather than growth rescuing governments from their fiscal predicaments, resolving fiscal imbalances through proactive and credible policies is likely to create better conditions for accelerating future economic growth.

Policy possibilities for the long term

How might fiscal imbalances be resolved in the future? There are several possibilities to consider. Firstly, most of the explicit debt is not inflation-linked and is therefore subject to erosion through higher inflation. The US Federal Reserve System, however, is appropriately wary of losing credibility as an inflation fighter – there is too much at stake, including the status of the dollar as the world's reserve currency. Similarly, the European Central Bank appears to have committed over the longer term to a firm anti-inflationary policy stance, knowing full well the high costs and difficulties of reversing an inflationary spiral should one take hold. In any case, as Table 5 and Figure 11 show, the share of explicit debt in total public indebtedness – debt that could be devalued through faster inflation – is relatively small in most countries.

To the extent that most of existing fiscal imbalances includes future inflation-protected social protection, inflationary public finance would be ineffective in reducing them. Of course, inflation protection on social expenditure programmes could be removed, but it would be a blunt instrument for achieving the goal of reducing future budget shortfalls and is likely to be politically unpopular as it would hurt pensioners who would be left on fixed incomes the most. That leaves only direct, progressive benefit reductions or tax increases as ways for resolving in-built future structural budget shortfalls that the fiscal imbalances reported here mainly represent. This approach can take a variety of forms such as the raising of the pension age, requiring higher participation in paying for non-catastrophic health expenses, extending the tax base in various ways by reducing exemptions and deductions, shifting younger generations to self- and pre-funded retirement and health systems, increasing the efficiency of government health systems, and so on. The extent to which taxes and spending would have to change in different countries is indicated in the analysis above. Nevertheless, such action would be unpopular with electorates, so what would force such action by policymakers?

There is a contradiction between the short-term imperative of boosting the economy, which some believe can be achieved through higher government expenditures financed by borrowing even more, and the necessary policy adjustments required over the long term on both the fiscal and monetary policy fronts. Fiscal policymakers abhor tax increases and spending reductions because of the implications of those policies for short-term economic growth and the direct negative effects on their constituents. The same appears to be true for monetary policy: in a manner similar to the Federal Reserve, the Bank of England recently provided forward guidance on monetary policy – tying it to a target unemployment rate – a policy that could be easily extended for too long despite its obvious negative implications for keeping inflation in check for the long term. The UK monetary policy announcement does, however, show that policymakers appreciate the importance of policy stability for boosting market confidence by enabling participants to plan for the future. A similar approach by fiscal authorities – through pro-active announcements about the path of future fiscal adjustments could act as a force-multiplier for market stability, consumer and investor confidence, and economic growth. Long-term fiscal stability is needed. This can only be achieved by using long-term fiscal metrics by which to judge policy and take timely policy action involving a planned scaling back of future health and social protection expenditure.

12 CONCLUSION

As far as the long-term resolution of fiscal imbalances is concerned, one can only envisage a repeat of the experience that several EU nations have already been through. On both sides of the Atlantic, budget deficits may increase continually as government expenditures on health care and public pensions spiral. As debt-to-GDP ratios increase further, investor confidence in government commitments to repay debts would erode, inducing capital flight and placing considerably greater upward pressure on interest rates. As some EU countries have already experienced, such developments on a wider scale would force painful but unavoidable fiscal consolidations.

However, rather than allow financial markets to force such a course of action with unpredictable results for ordinary citizens, it would be better to anticipate these problems and seek a more controlled resolution of national fiscal imbalances by political leaders in both the US and the EU. This is an approach that would be more likely to pay off in terms of faster future economic growth. The key is not just producing the right economic policies, but also solutions to the political prisoner's dilemma problem outlined above. This includes placing constraints on national budget processes to prevent excessive increases in not just explicit debt but in the sum of explicit and implicit debt.

The situation we face at the moment is that the accumulation of large fiscal obligations appears to be creating a policy freeze with opposing political interest groups hardening their policy positions. Growing distrust among law makers and an increasingly pejorative connotation applied to the term 'compromise' in the political sphere is progressively increasing the stakes. But this situation will magnify market uncertainty about the likely future policy course, causing investment to seize and economic growth to stall. A vicious cycle between growing fiscal imbalances, hardening political gridlock and slower economic growth appears to be developing with policymakers always seeking to postpone the required 'grand bargain'. Not surprisingly, we have witnessed the partial delegation by the US Congress of the task of managing fiscal policy to the Federal Reserve. But its quantitative easing policy of the last three years only appears to be destroying productive capital and employment through financial repression.

Given the starting point, it seems unlikely that lawmakers will find the will to make a direct quantum leap towards considerably reduced fiscal imbalances. Consider that, in the case of the US, a $91.4 trillion fiscal imbalance accruing interest costs at the government's long-term average borrowing rate of 3.6 per cent per year implies an annual cost accrual of $3.3 trillion dollars. Thus, the service cost of the outstanding US fiscal imbalance alone equals 21.2 per cent of annual GDP. Direct real and market-imposed adjustments of this magnitude are currently visible in EU nations such as Spain and Greece.

Whether a similar fate awaits the rest of the developed world or whether policymakers will find a sensible compass for navigating a less volatile course remains to be seen. The most sensible place to start the reform process would be at the evaluation stage. The starting point for good policy must be to adopt appropriate forward-oriented metrics of structural public-sector indebtedness. This involves adopting longer time horizons and a better, generational- and forward-oriented budget policy evaluation process. Clear accounting and reporting on the current policy path using the fiscal vocabulary of fiscal and generational imbalances and generational accounting is needed. The next step would be to design budget process reforms for constraining budget appropriations with particular benchmarks to be achieved over time. Those benchmarks must acknowledge the needs of current older generations who are ill-prepared for retirement and the requirements of stable fiscal policies that will not unduly burden younger generations. Younger people must face a policy environment in which saving and investment are encouraged to meet future pension and health-care needs which will also improve future prospects for economic growth.

The United States

This monograph was researched and written during mid 2013. This was six months after the US Congress decided to sidestep the 'fiscal cliff' problem in keeping with practice during the last several years. The final revisions were made during the government 'shutdown'. The problems that led to that shutdown have been postponed rather than resolved. The end result of the negotiations to sidestep the fiscal cliff was a cut in government spending of $1.2 trillion and the permanent extension of substantial George W. Bush era tax cuts (except the two-year-old partial employee payroll tax cut). These and other changes made earlier tax concessions permanent and postponed implementation of several scheduled fiscal policies to avoid imposing higher tax burdens on particular voter groups. This move from 'baseline' (or current) fiscal policies towards 'alternative' fiscal policies (or to past fiscal practice) implies an increase in the nation's fiscal imbalance by almost $26 trillion. Furthermore, it remains unclear how durable the $1.2 trillion sequester government spending cuts will prove to be.[3]

The US Congress therefore appears to be hewing closely to the alternative fiscal trajectory that, ironically, is likely to generate the same economic problems of high unemployment and stagnant or declining GDP growth that postponing tax increases and spending cuts is intended to avoid. Businesses and households will modify their economic choices in anticipation of even larger economically burdensome fiscal policy changes in the future. Current fiscal practice thus grants additional public goods and services

---

3   The Bipartisan Budget Act of 2013 (December) rolled back the spending sequester by $63 billion over two years – 2014–15 – and offset that change by saving in other parts of the federal budget. However, this two year agreement may mean no action on the larger debt reduction measures needed to make progress in resolving the US fiscal imbalance.

to Americans, but requires them to pay fewer taxes while allowing them to receive more in transfers – to the tune of about $32,000 for today's working men and $20,000 for today's working women – over the next ten years. If those policies are continued beyond the next ten years, those cohorts' benefits would be as large as $108,000 and $59,000, respectively, over their remaining lifetimes.

The fiscal and generational imbalances estimated in this study show the US to be hugely over-extended fiscally, with inherited debt plus future spending set to outpace revenues during coming decades. The US fiscal imbalance under the CBO's more realistic alternative projections equals 9 per cent of the nation's future GDP. The fiscal imbalance equals almost 20 per cent of the nation's wage base, implying that today's Social Security and Medicare payroll taxes would have to be more than doubled to resolve it. Alternatively, it will require a near doubling of federal income taxes that are levied on the nation's broadest tax base.

Under the CBO's alternative projections, two thirds of the overall US fiscal imbalance is accounted for by the fiscal imbalances in Social Security and Medicare, the nation's two largest entitlement programmes that provide pension and health care benefits to retirees, the disabled and their dependants and survivors. A subset of the imbalance in these two programmes is made up of scheduled benefits in excess of past payroll taxes by past generations and those alive today. Net social insurance obligations (benefit promises in excess of future payroll taxes) to today's generations equal $65 trillion but social insurance programme trust funds have just $2.9 trillion in them. That amounts to a funding ratio of just 4.8 per cent. Given that trust funds contain just paper 'IOUs' of the US Treasury, those resources must also be raised from future taxpayers. Thus, unless current social insurance policies are changed soon to resolve this 'generational imbalance', its funding burden will be transferred to future generations.

The transfer of such a large fiscal burden to future generations implies a transfer of wealth from future generations to living generations, especially to older living generations. Such transfers are clearly exerting real effects on today's generations' consumption choices as measured by the relative increase in consumption spending by older (versus younger) generations. A secular, fiscally induced, increase in consumption spending by current generations during the last several decades is the key likely explanation for the sustained decline in US national saving. That decline, in turn, is likely to constrain capital formation and future labour productivity and further impoverish younger and future generations.

The European Union

Similar remarks apply to many EU nations, albeit their governance and fiscal frameworks are considerably different from those in the US. The twin transitions that EU nations are undergoing – of demographic change and monetary union – were interrupted by the recession of 2008–9, one that is still ongoing in several major EU countries. The recession has worsened the policy trade-off that EU nations are facing as they try to ensure sustainable fiscal policies and an environment conducive to more rapid economic growth.

Under an expanded framework of budget accounting and with projections extended through to the year 2060, the fiscal imbalances of EU nations are found to average 13.5 per cent of their future GDP. EU nations' budget projections reveal expenditure commitments that are about 26 per cent larger than could be funded out of prospective government receipts. The recent recession has doubtless made it more difficult for countries to adopt fiscal policies to restore EU budgets to long-term sustainability. However, one reason for the delay in the return to sustainable fiscal policies may be the continuing practice of judging fiscal convergence on traditional deficit and debt measures that do not fully reflect the extent of accruing costs from structural fiscal shortfalls and future commitments made by government.

This monograph argues that the EU's fiscal policy-makers and practitioners should adopt the more comprehensive fiscal imbalance measure for judging national fiscal sustainability. Such measures reflect the long-term implications of current policies and consistently and comprehensively reflect changes in the government's financial condition resulting from any and every alternative tax and spending policy change. Moreover, the measures discussed in this monograph can potentially be used to assess the relative contributions to the overall fiscal imbalance from several underlying sources such as demographic structures, productivity growth, interest rates, budget structures and generational transfers embedded in budget plans.

The fiscal constraints facing EU countries – in terms of large required policy changes to cover future unfunded expenditure commitments – suggest that EU nations may be compelled to eventually reduce dependence on government-provided services significantly. This is especially so when it comes to social protection services. Instead, there needs to be greater reliance on alternative private sources of retirement and health support – including savings, insurance and employer provision. Without such reforms, the already hugely under-funded government provision of social insurance is likely to run aground, worsening the prospects for a successful economic and monetary union in Europe. The fiscal position of EU countries also bodes ill for their long-term growth prospects and the economic well-being of future generations.

REFERENCES

Abel, A. B., Mankiw, N. G., Summers, L. H. and Zeckhauser, R. J. (1989), 'Assessing dynamic efficiency: theory and evidence', National Bureau of Economic Research, Working Paper 2097.

Auerbach, A. J. and Kotlikoff, L. J. (1987), *Dynamic Fiscal Policy*, Cambridge, UK: Cambridge University Press.

Auerbach, A. J., Gokhale, J. and Kotlikoff, L. J. (1991), 'Generational accounts: a meaningful alternative to deficit accounting', *Tax Policy and the Economy*, Vol. 5, Cambridge, MA: MIT Press.

Auerbach, A. J., Gokhale, J., Kotlikoff, L. J. and Weil, D. N. (2001), 'The annuitization of Americans' resources: a cohort analysis', in L. J. Kotlikoff (ed.), *Essays on Savings, Bequests, Inequality, Altruism, and Life-Cycle Planning*, Cambridge, MA: MIT Press.

Congressional Budget Office (2012), 'Updated Budget Projections: Fiscal Years 2012–2022', March.

Congressional Budget Office (2012), 'The 2012 Long Term Budget Outlook', June.

Congressional Budget Office (2013), 'Updated Budget Projections: Fiscal Years 2013–2023', May.

Congressional Budget Office (1999), 'Economic and Budget Outlook: An Update', July.

Eurostat: National Accounts and Government Finance Statistics, available at http://epp.eurostat.ec.europa.eu/portal/page/portal/national_accounts/introduction.

Feldstein, M. S. (1974), 'Social security, induced retirement, and aggregate capital accumulation', *Journal of Political Economy*, 82(5): 905–26.

Gokhale, J. and Smetters, K. (2003), *Fiscal and Generational Imbalances: New Budget Measures for New Budget Priorities*, Washington, DC: AEI Press.

Gokhale, J. (2008), 'Entry on "generational accounting",' in S. N. Durlauf and L. E. Blume (ed.), *The New Palgrave Dictionary of Economics*, 2nd edn. Basingstoke, UK: Palgrave Macmillan.

Government Printing Office of the United States (2013), *Economic Report of the President*.

Government Printing Office of the United States (2012), *Annual Report of the Medicare Trustees*.

Government Printing Office of the United States (2014), 'The Budget of the United States Government, Fiscal Year 2014', Office of Management and Budget, April.

ABOUT THE IEA

The Institute is a research and educational charity (No. CC 235 351), limited by guarantee. Its mission is to improve understanding of the fundamental institutions of a free society by analysing and expounding the role of markets in solving economic and social problems.

The IEA achieves its mission by:

- a high-quality publishing programme
- conferences, seminars, lectures and other events
- outreach to school and college students
- brokering media introductions and appearances

The IEA, which was established in 1955 by the late Sir Antony Fisher, is an educational charity, not a political organisation. It is independent of any political party or group and does not carry on activities intended to affect support for any political party or candidate in any election or referendum, or at any other time. It is financed by sales of publications, conference fees and voluntary donations.

In addition to its main series of publications the IEA also publishes a quarterly journal, *Economic Affairs*.

The IEA is aided in its work by a distinguished international Academic Advisory Council and an eminent panel of Honorary Fellows. Together with other academics, they review prospective IEA publications, their comments being passed on anonymously to authors. All IEA papers are therefore subject to the same rigorous independent refereeing process as used by leading academic journals.

IEA publications enjoy widespread classroom use and course adoptions in schools and universities. They are also sold throughout the world and often translated/reprinted.

Since 1974 the IEA has helped to create a worldwide network of 100 similar institutions in over 70 countries. They are all independent but share the IEA's mission.

Views expressed in the IEA's publications are those of the authors, not those of the Institute (which has no corporate view), its Managing Trustees, Academic Advisory Council members or senior staff.

Members of the Institute's Academic Advisory Council, Honorary Fellows, Trustees and Staff are listed on the following page.

The Institute gratefully acknowledges financial support for its publications programme and other work from a generous benefaction by the late Alec and Beryl Warren.

The Institute of Economic Affairs
2 Lord North Street, Westminster, London SW1P 3LB
Tel: 020 7799 8900
Fax: 020 7799 2137
Email: iea@iea.org.uk
Internet: iea.org.uk

Other papers recently published by the IEA include:

Taxation and Red Tape
The Cost to British Business of Complying with the UK Tax System
Francis Chittenden, Hilary Foster & Brian Sloan
Research Monograph 64; ISBN 978-0-255-36612-0; £12.50

Ludwig von Mises – A Primer
Eamonn Butler
Occasional Paper 143; ISBN 978-0-255-36629-8; £7.50

Does Britain Need a Financial Regulator?
Statutory Regulation, Private Regulation and Financial Markets
Terry Arthur & Philip Booth
Hobart Paper 169; ISBN 978-0-255-36593-2; £12.50

Hayek's The Constitution of Liberty
An Account of Its Argument
Eugene F. Miller
Occasional Paper 144; ISBN 978-0-255-36637-3; £12.50

Fair Trade Without the Froth
A Dispassionate Economic Analysis of 'Fair Trade'
Sushil Mohan
Hobart Paper 170; ISBN 978-0-255-36645-8; £10.00

A New Understanding of Poverty
Poverty Measurement and Policy Implications
Kristian Niemietz
Research Monograph 65; ISBN 978-0-255-36638-0; £12.50

The Challenge of Immigration
A Radical Solution
Gary S. Becker
Occasional Paper 145; ISBN 978-0-255-36613-7; £7.50

Sharper Axes, Lower Taxes
Big Steps to a Smaller State
Edited by Philip Booth
Hobart Paperback 38; ISBN 978-0-255-36648-9; £12.50

Self-employment, Small Firms and Enterprise
Peter Urwin
Research Monograph 66; ISBN 978-0-255-36610-6; £12.50

Other IEA publications

Comprehensive information on other publications and the wider work of the IEA can be found at www.iea.org.uk. To order any publication please see below.

Personal customers

Orders from personal customers should be directed to the IEA:

Clare Rusbridge
IEA
2 Lord North Street
FREEPOST LON10168
London SW1P 3YZ
Tel: 020 7799 8907. Fax: 020 7799 2137
Email: sales@iea.org.uk

Trade customers

All orders from the book trade should be directed to the IEA's distributor:

NBN International (IEA Orders)
Orders Dept.
NBN International
10 Thornbury Road
Plymouth PL6 7PP
Tel: 01752 202301, Fax: 01752 202333
Email: orders@nbninternational.com

IEA subscriptions

The IEA also offers a subscription service to its publications. For a single annual payment (currently £42.00 in the UK), subscribers receive every monograph the IEA publishes. For more information please contact:

Clare Rusbridge
Subscriptions
IEA
2 Lord North Street
FREEPOST LON10168
London SW1P 3YZ
Tel: 020 7799 8907, Fax: 020 7799 2137
Email: crusbridge@iea.org.uk